ABOUT THE AUTHOR

KEITH G. RICHARDS owns and operates
ValueTrend Wealth Management (sponsoring investment dealer
Worldsource Securities Inc., Member – Canadian Investor Protection
Fund), where he is a discretionary Portfolio Manager for high-net-worth
clients. Keith has been in the securities industry since 1990 and appears
often on BNN, CTV's Business News Network, as an author and popular
media personality. He writes for a number of financial publications
including *Globe and Mail, Toronto Star, Financial Post (National
Post), The MoneyLetter,* and *Investor's Digest of Canada.* Keith is
certified as a Chartered Market Technician (CMT), the benchmark
designation for Technical Analysts. He is also an accredited CIM
(Certified Investment Manager) and FCSI (Fellow of the
Canadian Securities Institute).

SIDEWAYS

Using the Power of Technical Analysis to Profit in Uncertain Times

Keith G. Richards

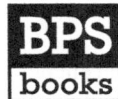

BPS books

Toronto and New York
www.bpsbooks.com

Published in 2011 by
BPS Books
Toronto and New York
www.bpsbooks.com
A division of Bastian Publishing Services Ltd.

ISBN 978-1-926645-68-1

Cataloguing-in-Publication Data available from Library
and Archives Canada.

Front cover design and diagrams: Kimberly Viney
Interior design and typesetting: Daniel Crack, KD Books, www.kdbooks.ca
Cover photograph: Mike Guilbault Photography

To my wife, Jane:

Thank you for your support
on those weekends and vacation days
when I mysteriously
vanished to work on this book

CONTENTS

INTRODUCTION

Markets Can Go Sideways

IN my first book, *SmartBounce: 3 Action Steps to Portfolio Recovery*, I showed that the major U.S. stock markets have been stuck in a trading range since 1999. As we have seen from the Dow and S&P 500, they have hit both a floor and a ceiling. A market contained within a trading range can be called a *sideways market*. I suggested in *SmartBounce* that this sideways market will likely continue until somewhere in the middle of the current decade – perhaps 2015 or later.

Charles Dow began tracking stock market data in the late 1880s to create the Dow Jones Industrial Average, or DJIA. Figure 1 shows the entire history of the DJIA. I've added horizontal lines to the chart to mark periods occurring on the Dow during that time. You can see the current sideways period at the far right side of the chart, where it is marked by a horizontal line. Notice how these sideways periods often last about 15 to 17 years before a new bull market begins. I continue to believe the current sideways market, which began in 1999, could remain in force until 2015 or later.

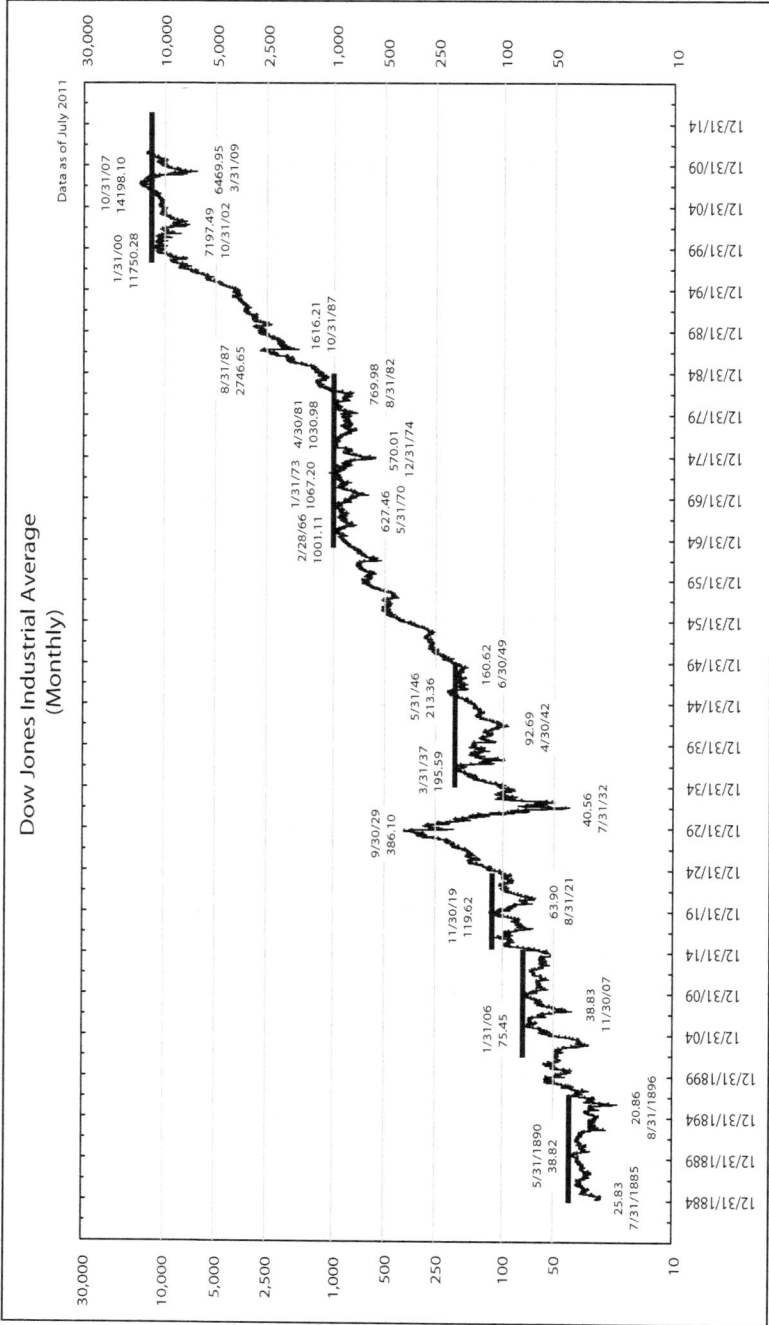

Figure 1. Dow Jones Industrial Average from the 1880s with sideways periods. (Copyright © 2010 Thechartstore.com)

In the spring of 2011, as I was writing this book, the market had just moved close to the top of its trading range at a little over Dow 12000. As an investor, I follow the strategy I will outline for you in this book. So when the Dow broke above 12000 and the S&P 500 approached 1,400, in conjunction with other bearish technical and fundamental signals that I will explain later, I went into action by reducing equities. After all, in March 2009 the few investors who had the nerve and experience to buy at the bottom were rewarded with a phenomenal 90% return when the market recovered from its low point.

Importantly, a strong stock market recovery, like the one from March 2009, almost always increases investors' appetite for risk. During strong markets, more and more investors join the bullish herd expecting greater and greater returns in the future. One key thing for you to learn from this book is how to identify when investors have become too bullish and the herd is about to be stopped. We'll cover specific sentiment-based indicators to identify these periods of excess bullishness. For now, realize that the greatest fortunes are made by investors who aren't afraid of stepping away from the herd and taking a contrary position.

Why should the markets continue to trade in a sideways range for the next number of years? Aren't things rebuilding? Aren't corporate profits rising? Isn't consumer confidence returning to normal? Hasn't the stock market recovered from its March 2009 lows of below Dow 7000 (and 800 on the S&P 500)? It's no coincidence that these levels represent the bottom trading range I outlined in *SmartBounce*.

Some market analysts like to compare the current environment in North America with that of Japan in the late 1980s and early 1990s. There certainly are some points of comparison in the chart patterns. Figure 2 is a chart of Japan's Nikkei 225 going back to 1970. After the initial Japanese stock market crash that ended in 1992, the Nikkei rebounded from its low level of 14000 back to 22000 within a year. Just as we saw with the North American market rebound, the Nikkei's bounce represented a return of about 60% for investors who had the foresight to buy at the bottom.

But this is all that buy-and-hold investors have been able to squeeze out of Japan's forlorn stock market since that initial recovery almost 20 years ago. To this day, the Nikkei trades at about one quarter of its peak value of 1990. It has moved in a downward sloping trading direction since then. I've marked that slope on the chart with a black trendline.

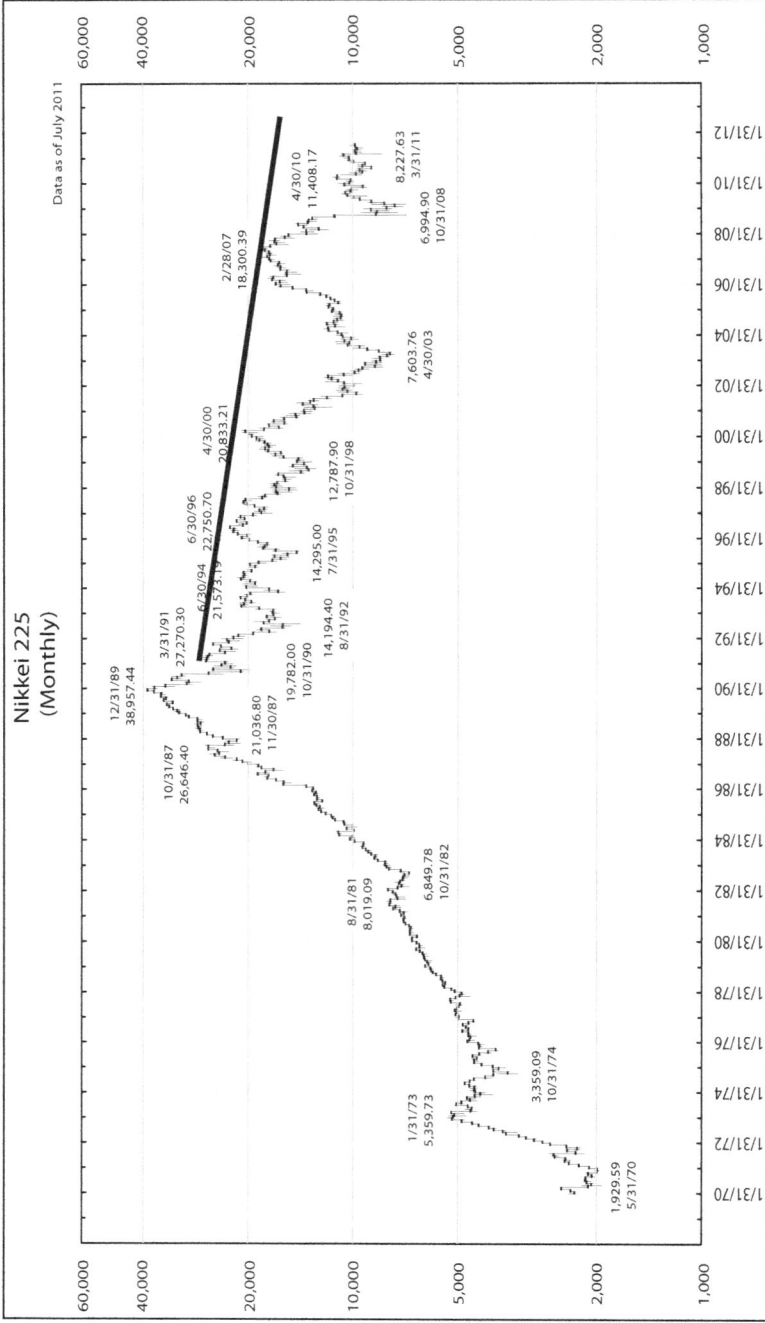

Figure 2. Nikkei 1970 to now. (Copyright © 2010 Thechartstore.com)

Why might the U.S. markets behave as Japan's market has over the past 20 years? For one thing, the U.S. relies on consumers to drive its economy, just as Japan did during the 1980s. Unfortunately, the U.S. consumer is not likely to return any time soon to the consumption-driven mentality that drove stock markets higher during the 1982-1999 bull market or during the 2007 bubble peak. Why? Well, calculations made by Ross Healy of Strategic Analysis Corporation (SAC) suggest that the balance sheet of the U.S. consumer alone is overextended by about $6 trillion. And he calculates that the U.S. economy can efficiently support a total debt load of about *$21 trillion*. That's approximately $1.45 to $1.50 per dollar of GDP. Instead, total U.S. indebtedness totals more than *$52 trillion*. It's over twice the level it should be. Healy believes the U.S. economy is approaching a financially insolvent situation.

Further, the U.S. is not the only country facing these problems. There are debt repayment and recovery challenges facing a large number of countries, including the European PHIGS (Portugal, Hungary, Italy, Ireland, Greece, and Spain). Nonetheless, the U.S. debt situation may well be the major contributor to the current sideways market. To understand more about debt and inflation, read J. Anthony Boeckh's outstanding book *The Great Reflation*. This book explains the historical rise of debt and inflation since the early 1900s and why modern governments have difficulty dealing with them.

I'm often asked by the financial press what catalysts might underlie the various market changes I'm predicting. For instance, in May 2011 I elected to reduce some equities in the accounts I manage. I suggested to a Business News Network (BNN) television audience at the time that investors start to sell some equities and reallocate this capital into cash. This inspired the BNN host to ask if the then-current pressing issues surrounding Middle East revolutions and similar political struggles throughout the world were driving my bearish viewpoint. I explained that the potential topping (and subsequent decline) of the stock markets over the coming months would not be the result of what's in the headlines but of the level of fear or greed in the market, which can be spotted in the chart patterns. People often find this viewpoint difficult to accept. They want to see a tangible reason for a selloff or rally.

When markets are trading at certain very high levels, they are referred to as being overvalued or overbought. When they are trading at certain very low levels, they are referred to as being undervalued or oversold. These terms almost speak for themselves, though I'll spend some time explaining them in detail later in this book. When markets are overbought or oversold, it really doesn't matter what sparks the subsequent selloff or rally. Market participants in the know will actively be looking for overbought or oversold conditions. When they find them, they'll begin selling stocks or accumulating stocks respectively.

Like a party balloon, the market can be underinflated (undervalued) or overinflated (overvalued). When the balloon gets too big, or overinflated, it takes only a small nick or a slight bump to break it. Somebody walks by the balloon and brushes it with a button on his shirtsleeve and *boom* – the balloon pops. Was the guy with the shirtsleeve careless? Should he be blamed for breaking the balloon? Or was the balloon too big to begin with and about to burst anyway?

The truth is, it doesn't matter what broke the balloon. Markets, like balloons, can and do become too inflated at times. If you use the tools outlined in this book, you'll have a better chance of being *out* of the markets when things get overinflated and *in* the markets when things look attractive again. In other words, as a smaller, nimbler investor, you'll learn how to make and keep profit in a sideways trading environment.

I've designed this book as an introduction to technical analysis for the retail investor and will also touch on a few key areas of fundamental analysis. Technical analysis offers investors and traders an important advantage for profiting in the current market environment. It's the only mechanism that allows you to quantitatively and qualitatively measure the emotions of market participants and profit by them. My philosophy is to have you profit by, rather than be a victim of, a range-bound trading environment.

I've tried to make *Sideways*, like *SmartBounce*, a pragmatic book. It focuses on tools to help you start winning the investment game right away. You'll benefit from the knowledge gained over my 20-plus years of experience in the investment industry. In my early years, I made every mistake possible. But in doing so, I learned to decipher clues that now allow me to profitably respond to the stock market's daily changes.

Through *Sideways,* you're going to learn to decipher these clues yourself. You'll learn an investment strategy that will reduce your risk and increase your profitability on the stock market. You'll learn to remove your emotions from your trading decisions. Finally, you'll learn to focus on following a proven, disciplined buy-and-sell decision-making system. Honestly, I wish someone had written this book 20 years ago so I could have operated as efficiently on the markets then as I do now.

Before we get started, I'd like to stress that *Sideways* has been written for stock market participants who wish to follow a defensive strategy in the current volatile range-bound trading environment. It will not appeal to aggressive investors or the get-rich-quick crowd.

There are many types of trading strategies. Some are geared toward the short-term trader. For example, swing trading can be an effective tool for traders with an intraday focus – those who are trading in and out over just a few hours or days. This book is not for them. Similarly, there are longer-term investing systems such as in-depth fundamental analysis, Elliott Wave Theory, or Gann analysis. These may be too complex or time-consuming for the average retail investor to learn to use effectively. Although we will be discussing a few of the usable applications derived from these analytical tools, for the most part these methodologies are too esoteric for the average investor.

In contrast to both of these approaches, I want to share with you practical tools from the field of technical analysis that I have found to make money. In other words, I'm going to provide you with the real meat and potatoes part of your investment strategy meal.

In the first four chapters of this book, I cover the basics of technical analysis and help you see why it works. I explore trends, market phases, formations, and cycles and how to profit by them. I address how you can time your entry and exit points on the market. From there I'll show you how to tweak those entry and exit points through technical indicators. These will clarify what you see on the charts.

In chapters 5 and 6, I look at broad market timing tools. These will help you decide whether to overweight or underweight equities in your portfolio according to time-tested indicators and market cycles.

In chapter 8, I introduce you to Japanese candlestick charting – again, helping you to determine if and when the timing is right for buying and selling individual securities.

Finally, I pull it all together by visiting a fictional character who utilizes the lessons learned in *Sideways*. While the character is fictional, the trades and observations he makes were actually made during 2010.

They were executed in real time by me acting in the capacity of Portfolio Manager for my firm, ValueTrend Wealth Management.

Sideways focuses not on every known technical analysis technique or tool available for analyzing securities but on the most practical tools I have found – tools to assist the majority of retail investors making buy-and-sell decisions in the current investment climate.

Let's get started.

1

PHASES

HUMAN beings go through many stages of life: childhood, adolescence, parenthood, old age, and death. Similarly, the market goes through its own life stages. We call them phases. By understanding the market's phases, you'll be able to identify its current status and how to trade profitably.

Early in my career, I was privileged to be taught the basics of technical analysis by one of the greatest market technicians of our time, Ralph Acampora. In his teachings, Ralph illustrated that all securities go through four distinct phases. Each phase has distinctive characteristics and each should be traded differently.

The phases are basing, bull market, topping, and bear market. I have discovered, through practical experience, that these four phases exist over various time frames. Day traders can identify these phases on an intraday chart, and longer-term traders can identify them over longer scales such as weekly or even monthly charts. Because most of you reading this book are likely mid- to long-term investors, I'm going to focus on the identification of these phases over longer periods.

However, the concept of each phase is the same for all time frames, including intraday patterns. It's vitally important for you to grasp the concepts laid out in this chapter. Only by recognizing which phase a security or broad market is in can you plan and execute a profitable trading strategy. In a later chapter I will present specific patterns associated with each of the four phases.

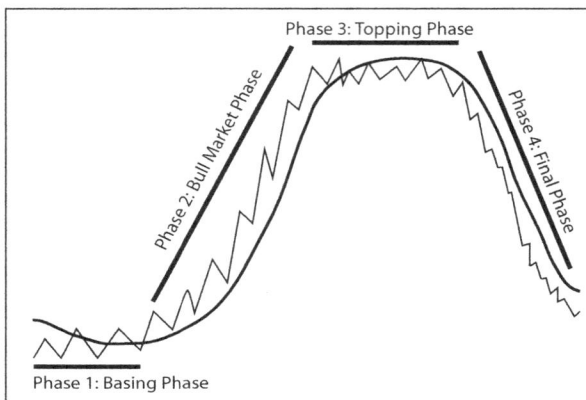

Figure 3. The four phases of securities.

Phase One: Basing Phase

In this phase, the market trades in a sideways pattern or forms some sort of bottoming pattern. Market participants move in equilibrium. The pattern does not always look like a precisely contained rectangle with defined upper (resistance) and lower (support) levels. Instead, it may exhibit a number of peaks and troughs. These create various bottom formations that Technical Analysts have identified over time. The basing phase may last for weeks or even months before breaking out into the next phase of the market. In sideways markets, indicators such as moving averages (which you will learn about later) tend to flatten out.

Typically, I avoid buying into a basing pattern unless it is a perfect rectangle with an easily identified support level (a level where the security tends to bounce up) – again, more on this later. The important thing is this: It's usually better not to buy a security during basing phase patterns but to stay on the sidelines and wait for it to break out into a new uptrend. I'll give you more tools in the next chapter for identifying a new trend.

No security remains in equilibrium forever. The very nature of a market is to be moving either up or down. Thus, volume tends to increase slowly during the basing phase. Informed buyers, whom I like to call "smart money," begin to pick up the stock from frustrated sellers who have lost faith in it. Trading volume is fairly low due to general lack of interest. When the security breaks out of a phase one consolidation pattern, it moves up through the overhead resistance level and, in the case of a daily chart, stays there for at least three days.

If the security does this with strong volume, it's about to move into the phase two bullish phase. I like to see, on encountering a phase one breakout, a spike of at least 50% in the trading volume. You can see this on the volume bars at the bottom of the chart. You'll learn more about identifying phase one bottoming patterns in a later chapter.

Phase one is the most attractive time to buy a market or security. As I mentioned earlier, I recommend you buy after you have seen a breakout from an overhead resistance level. Resistance, according to technical analysis, is an area where the security has had difficulty breaking through to the upside in the past – such as the ceiling I mentioned for the major U.S. stock markets over the past decade. I usually wait to see if the security price pulls back to the point where the stock broke through the resistance level. That's the perfect entry point.

Don't despair if you miss the pullback to old resistance or if it doesn't happen. Buy the stock anytime after you have established that it isn't likely to return to its former consolidation or basing pattern. See figure 7 on page 21 for a chart featuring Emera's breakout from a sideways consolidation. The stock broke through its old $23 resistance in the fall of 2009. It tested that area shortly after the breakout with a series of small rallies and pullbacks around $23. Then it moved into a phase two bull market.

Phase Two: Bull Market Phase

As mentioned, after the market breaks out of the basing phase, it typically pulls back briefly to the breakout point, sometimes called the neckline. I like to call this the neckline test. Wait to see the price pullback successfully bounce off the neckline before buying. If you're quick enough, you can buy the security very close to the neckline price as it bounces off. Again, don't fret if you miss those first few points and buy a bit higher.

The security then enters into a new phase of bullish price movement that usually lasts for many weeks or months. Along the way there are plenty of peaks and troughs to provide ample opportunity to time your entry point. As the market begins to move higher, draw a trendline connecting the first three rising troughs. Watch the moving averages for trend confirmation and enjoy the easy part of the ride. Keep in mind that the longer the trend has been in place, the more likely it is ready to change.

The angle of the trendline may begin to ascend at an even sharper angle after a while. It's a sure sign of a story that's about to end. Near the end of a phase two uptrend, peaks and troughs will become more erratic in their rhythm. The time elapsed between peaks will start to vary. Price movement between peaks and troughs becomes greater and greater. Volume may increase aggressively as the trend nears its end and the market is becoming overly confident about the long-term outlook. Eventually the market moves into a phase three topping pattern. It will soon be time to get out of your long positions.

Phase Three: Topping Phase

Like phase one, the topping phase is a trading-range market. But this phase occurs after a security has had a long bull run. The formations making up a phase three top are often a mirror image of phase one. Turn a phase one bottom pattern on its head and you have a phase three topping pattern.

At the end of an uptrend, there are many market participants. They have bought into the story of never-ending profits. Elliott Wave Theory (which will be covered briefly in a later chapter) might call this the fifth wave in an uptrend. Volume is high as the smart money begins to sell the stock to less discerning retail investors. There are still plenty of believers in the story, so markets churn aggressively up and down as shares rapidly change hands. News stories and earnings reports are favorable, supporting the conviction of the believers. It's almost a religious experience. Believers spread the word, converting skeptics into equally fanatic devotees of the bull market. Just as with phase one, all consolidation patterns cause moving-average lines to flatten out.

Eventually, the stronger, smart money people finish dumping their positions into weaker hands. Next, a piece of news or a fundamental event occurs, which triggers a sharp drop in price over a very confined period of time. Interestingly, such a piece of news might cause only a temporary disruption in the uptrend during a phase two bull market. During a typical bull market, such an interruption sees relatively low commitment verified by lower trading volume. But during the phase three topping phase of the market, the negative news event can create a dramatic drop in price supported by a spike in volume. The security breaks down through technical support (the neckline).

As with a phase one breakout, watch for the stock to stay below the neckline for at least three days. From there you'll usually see a test of the neckline in which the security makes a final rally back to its former support level. This is your final opportunity to sell out of the market. The security now moves into the bearish phase. Sell the security when it has broken the neckline, or hold at your own peril.

Phase Four: Final Phase

The final phase of a typical market pattern is the bearish phase. Just as phase three is the mirror image of phase one, the bearish phase of the market is a mirror image of the phase two bullish phase. The major difference between an uptrend and downtrend (beside the obvious directional trend) is the length of time. I don't know if any formal studies have been done on the subject of the timeframe for price trends. As a rule of thumb, downtrends for a given security usually last about one-third as long as the preview uptrend. Phase four downtrends, when compared with an uptrend, are fast and furious. If you're long in ownership of a particular security and don't recognize the symptoms of a phase three topping pattern, you'd better get with the program and sell quickly. Time is costing you money. With luck you won't stick around long enough to witness the three declining peaks and troughs that characterize a downtrend.

As described in our trend identification process, a trendline can be drawn connecting the tops of at least three peaks in a phase four downtrend. I personally don't short sell securities (i.e., selling a stock you don't own, hoping to buy it back later at a lower price). However, aggressive traders can identify points to short the market along the top of a declining trendline. If you are so inclined, you can sell short when the stock price hits the trendline. On the other hand, conservative investors who hold equities they've identified as being in a phase four bear market can consider using hedging or selling strategies to protect their portfolio at this stage.

Eventually, a phase four bear market ends, and a phase one basing pattern emerges. In the Disney classic *The Lion King*, Mufaso explains to his son that a caribou eats the grass. Then the lion eats the caribou. Finally the lion dies to feed the grass and complete the circle of life. The stock market, like all things, will complete its circle of life by moving through its four phases over and over again. The circle of life is inevitable in the wild. But when we trade on the stock market, we want to be in the security as it breaks out (phase one) and trends up (phase two). Then, we want to identify the third and fourth phases of the market in order to know when to sell. This is how to avoid becoming fodder for the strongest traders.

In a Nutshell

In this chapter you learned that markets move through four phases. They revolve through them on an ongoing basis like lions through the circle of life. These phases occur over both long and short time scales. It's key for you to identify the current phase of the market in order to be able to trade profitably in that market.

Phase one and phase three are similar in being transitional or reversal phases. The market is changing from a downtrend to an eventual uptrend during phase one. This is why I call it the basing phase. Phase three is the topping phase. Here the market transitions out of a bull market (uptrend) and reverses direction into a new bear market (downtrend). Learn to identify the basing and topping phases of the market. Failing to do so will result in missed opportunities (basing phase) or avoidable losses (topping phase).

Phases two and four are directional or trending phases. The market is in an uptrend during phase two. Obviously it pays to be long and stay in the market during this phase. Conversely, during phase four the market is in a downtrend. Out or short are the only tactics to consider during phase four.

The next two chapters introduce trend identification techniques and chart formations. These are known as chart patterns. They can help identify the current phase of the market so you can trade it effectively and profitably. The identification of chart patterns is one of the most interesting aspects of technical analysis.

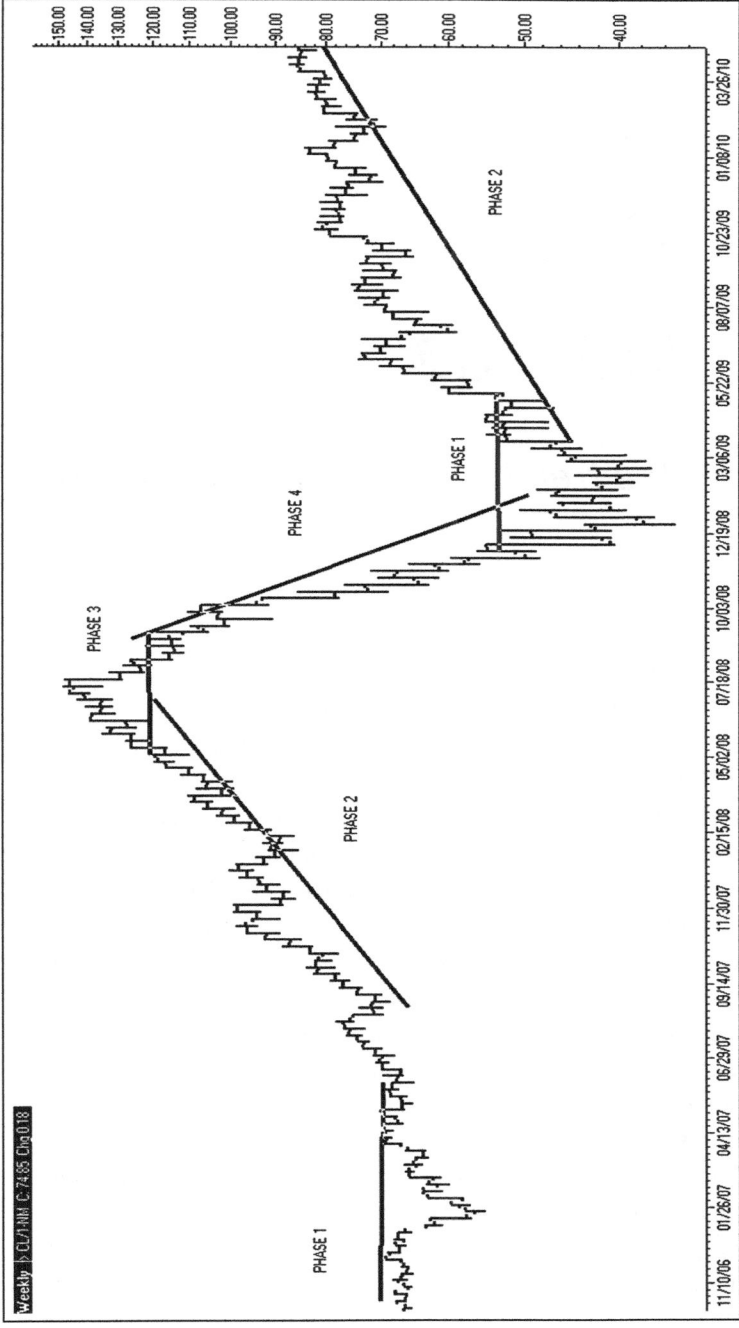

Figure 4. The four phases. Notice oil prices between late 2006 and early 2010. This is a beautiful illustration of the principles of rotation between the four phases of the market. (Copyright © 1988-2008, Thomson Financial)

PHASES

2

TRENDS

The trend is your friend, until the end

THE basic premise of technical analysis is that broad markets, commodities, and individual securities all move in price trends. These trends can take place on various timescales, from multi-year macro trends right down to intraday trends that may last only a few minutes. All trends occurring in securities markets result from how individuals trading in those markets react emotionally to events. That's the fear and greed I mentioned in the introduction.

Technical analysis shows us that it's not fundamental events such as earnings or breaking news but reactions to those events by the investing public and professionals that cause securities to rise or fall in price.

Events that can and will affect financial markets will change, but the reaction to those events will always be predictable.

People sometimes ask me if, given the changing world we live in, my rules for determining entry and exit points on the markets will stop working in the future. My answer is that the technical analysis tools I use will continue to work so long as human beings remain emotional creatures hardwired to move in herds. The herding tendency has been present in mankind since Homo sapiens first arose in Africa over 50,000 years ago. Why should that stop being so now?

There are many historical examples of investors moving in herds. They've driven stocks to bubble highs because of news and events that seemed to justify the hype. Recent examples include the stock market technology bubble/crash of 2001 and the commodity bubble/crash of 2008. Following any bubble, there is an equally frantic movement by the herd out of the market. This creates a downtrend. The selloffs following the technology and commodity bubbles were multi-month downtrends. Of course, they too ended. They eventually formed a bottom and turned up into a brand new uptrend.

Smart money profits by learning to identify how people instinctively move in herds. Investors and traders, driven by their emotions, create these trends through their mass movements in and out of securities. Once we learn how to identify these movements, we can jump in when the crowd begins to move into a market and exit when we see the trend coming to an end. More importantly, we can learn how to separate ourselves from our natural emotional tendency to follow the crowd. Instead, we can step outside our individual emotional reactions and exercise a quantitative approach to profit by the crowd's predictable patterns.

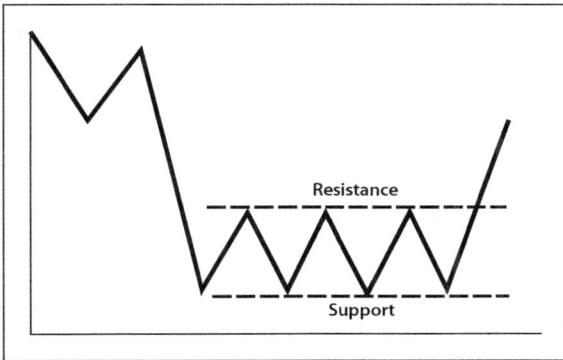

Figure 5. Technical resistance and technical support levels.

Support and Resistance

There are two key concepts to understand before we dive into the art of trend identification: the ideas of technical resistance and technical support levels. Resistance and support show up on stock charts because of one absolute reality in the markets: that all participants in the market, including sophisticated traders and less knowledgeable retail investors, are *human beings*.

Technical resistance: Humans are emotional creatures who have memories. People remember how much they paid for a stock that has since gone down in price. They want their money back. If the market returns to that level, they'll sell their securities to achieve that goal. If enough people sell at the same price level, this creates technical resistance. Selling pressure created by these traders tends to hold the stock back, providing resistance against further price gains. The more times the security rises and bounces down from this overhead price level, the more significant the level of resistance.

Technical support: People may have sold a stock or missed out on buying at a low level only to have seen it rise significantly. They remember that price level and wish they had bought or held the security at that point. Should the security reach this price again, they place their orders to buy. They don't want to miss out on the great opportunity they missed the first time. As buyers step in to accumulate the security at this favored price point, the security price bounces up.

We identify support and resistance on a chart by the number of times a security touches a certain price level.

If you notice an area where the security has hit a ceiling over and over again, you are looking at an area of resistance caused by the aforementioned sellers.

When you see there is some type of floor below which the security hesitates to go, you have identified an area of support.

The more tests, or places on the chart that touch these areas, the more significant the support or resistance level. I like to see at least two or three tests of a support or resistance level before I assign any significance to the price level in question. The volume bars, located at the bottom of your chart, can also give clues as to the strength or significance of the support or resistance level. Big spikes in volume occurring over and over at certain price points indicate that many sellers and buyers exchanged their positions at those levels.

Take a look at figure 6 on page 19. Notice where I've drawn levels of support and resistance for Emera, a Canadian electrical utility company,

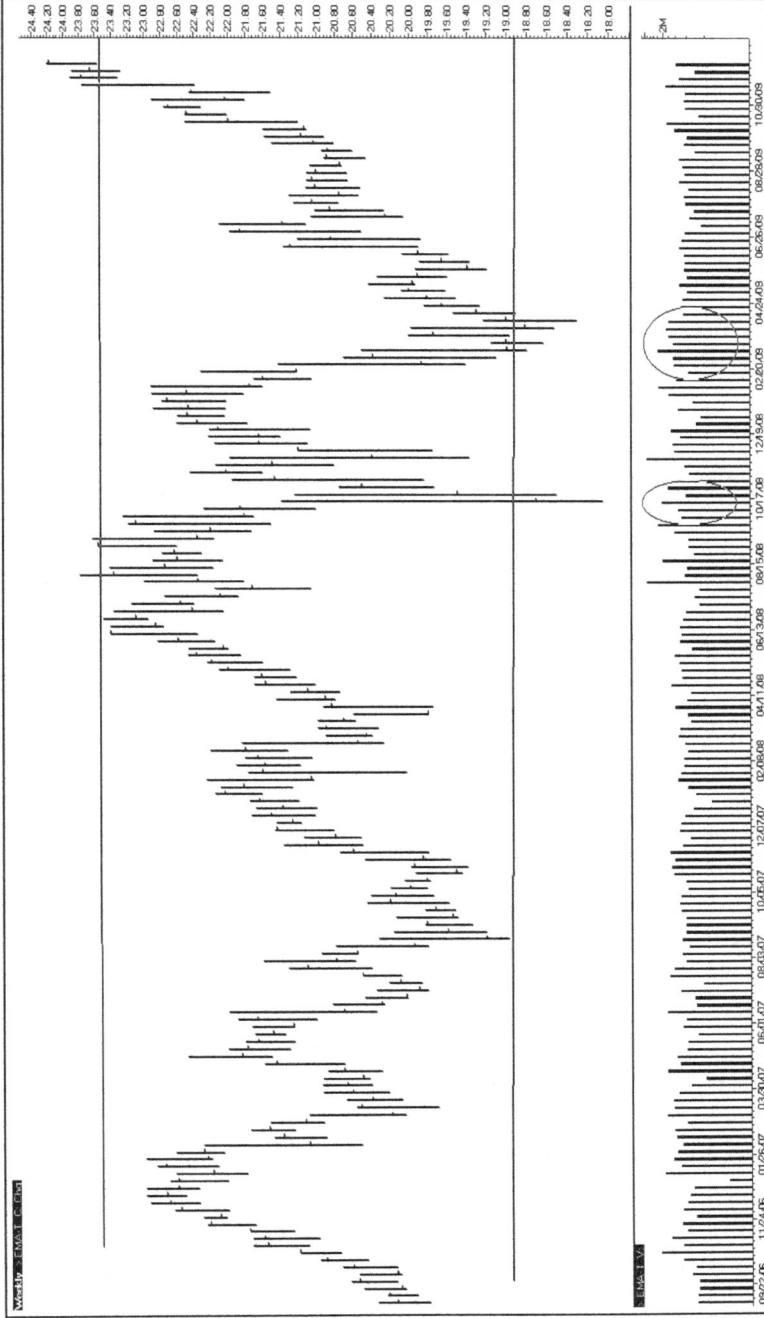

Figure 6. Chart of Emera with support and resistance. (Copyright © 1988-2008, Thomson Financial)

TRENDS

19

between November 2005 and the fall of 2009. The stock was stuck in a defined trading range between $18.50 and $23 during this period. Note the volume spikes, which I've circled, which provide further evidence for the significance of $18.50 as support. As a rule of thumb, we want to sell into resistance, anticipating that the stock will likely fall from that level and we want to buy at support, anticipating that the stock will likely rise from there.

Old Resistance Becomes New Support and Vice Versa

Recall that resistance is created by a group of investors who bought at a previously higher level on the market and now want to sell at that level to break even on the trade. This selling pressure creates a level of resistance for the security to break. Should the market break through this old resistance level and move on to higher levels, the former level of resistance typically becomes the new support level for the market.

Again, investors and traders are emotional. They tend to remember at what price they had previously sold. Now that the stock has gone up through the old resistance price level, they regret having sold where they did. As the security exhibits a pullback in price, the former sellers step in to accumulate shares. This causes the stock to rise from the old resistance level, turning that into the new support level.

As the pattern occurs over and over, new buyers appear who want to buy the security at the price they have seen it pulled back to a few times. Combined with the old sellers, these new buyers add further strength to the support level that has been created from old resistance. On the next Emera chart (figure 7), I've moved ahead in time to show you how the old resistance of $23 became the new support level after the stock was able to break up through $23.

The reverse occurs when old support becomes new resistance. Once a security price breaks down through the old support level, the former buyers who created that level of support want their money back. If the security rallies back to its former support level, they sell. As the security attempts to regain its positive upward momentum, old buyers who bought the security at the higher levels continue to sell with the objective of recovering their capital. New traders notice the tendency for the security to sell off at these levels. From this point forward, old support becomes the new resistance level.

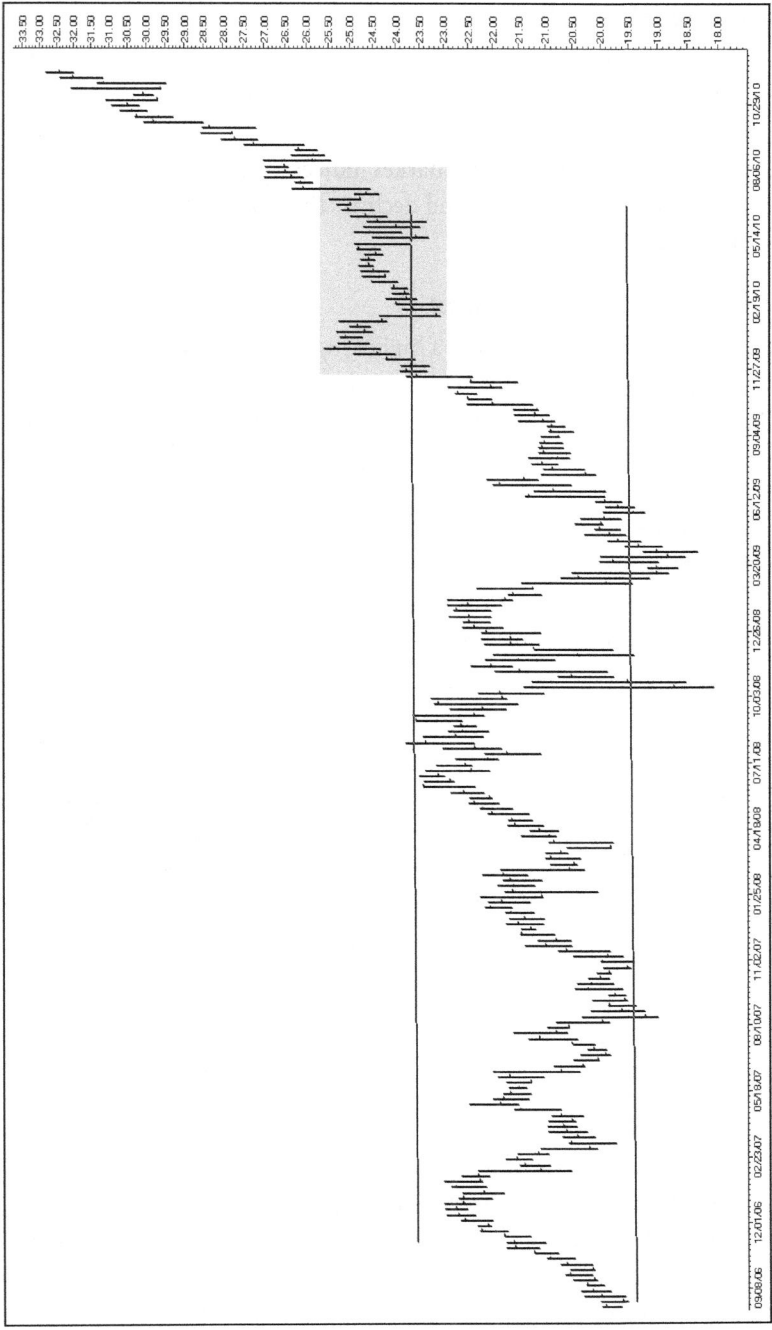

Figure 7. Chart of Emera resistance becoming support after breakout. (Copyright © 1988-2008, Thomson Financial)

TRENDS

Trending Markets

Markets can only move in one of three directions: *up*, *down*, or *sideways*. These three directions are trends. Let's examine how to quickly identify the trend of a security (or market).

Trends in securities or broad market indices are identified by the direction of the ongoing rallies and declines that naturally occur on all securities traded on a free market.

Uptrends and Downtrends

In an *uptrend*, each rally reaches a higher high than that of the last rally, and each decline (trough) stops at a level that's higher than the prior decline. When you can identify a series of at least three higher rallies and higher troughs in your given chart time, you can confirm that the stock is in an uptrend.

In a *downtrend*, each decline is lower and the rallies stop at a lower level than the previous rally. When you can identify a series of at least three lower rallies and lower troughs in your given chart time, you can confirm that the stock is in a downtrend.

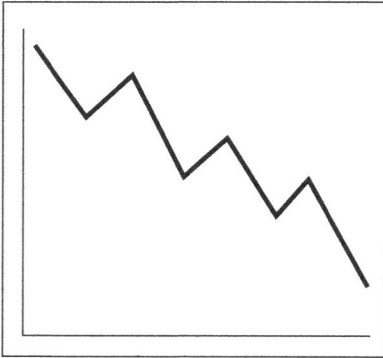

Figure 8. Downward trend.   Figure 9. Upward trend.

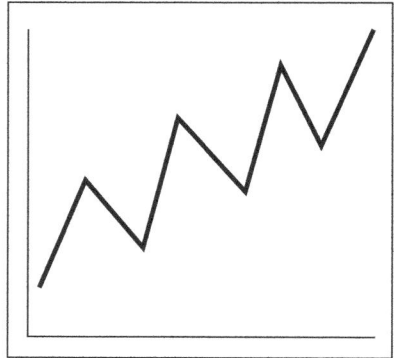

A useful habit to form is to draw trendlines on your chart when you identify an uptrend or downtrend on a security or market.

In an uptrend, draw your trendline underneath the price action on the chart. Start the trendline at the first trough and extend it to the third or most recent trough. Ideally, your trendline will touch or come very close to touching the middle troughs between the two extremes.

22

It's important to note the angle of your trendline. If it has a steep angle of ascent or descent, it may not last too much longer.

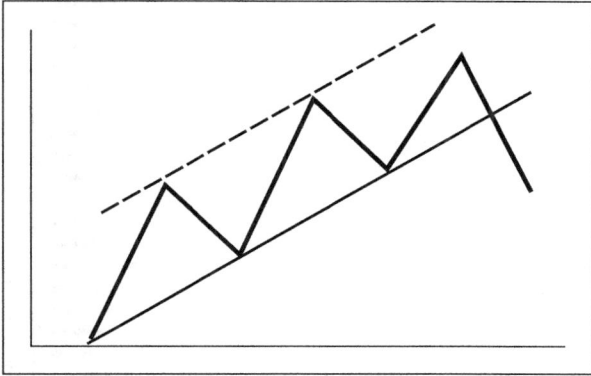

Figure 10. A trend channel up.

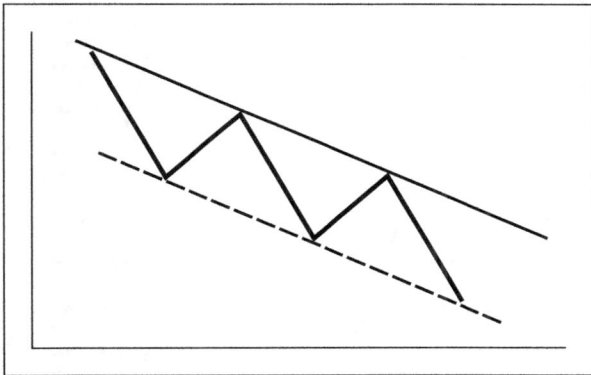

Figure 11. A trend channel down.

Conversely, a shallow trendline suggests that the trend may last awhile.

A steep trendline indicates that investors are either overly enthusiastic or overly pessimistic in their trading behavior.

A shallow trendline indicates a more orderly market, as opposed to a market fueled by extreme greed or fear, and is more likely to last awhile.

To identify a downtrend, look for at least three successive lower lows and lower rallies to establish the validity of the trend. Draw your trendline connecting three successively lower rallies to show the angle of descent.

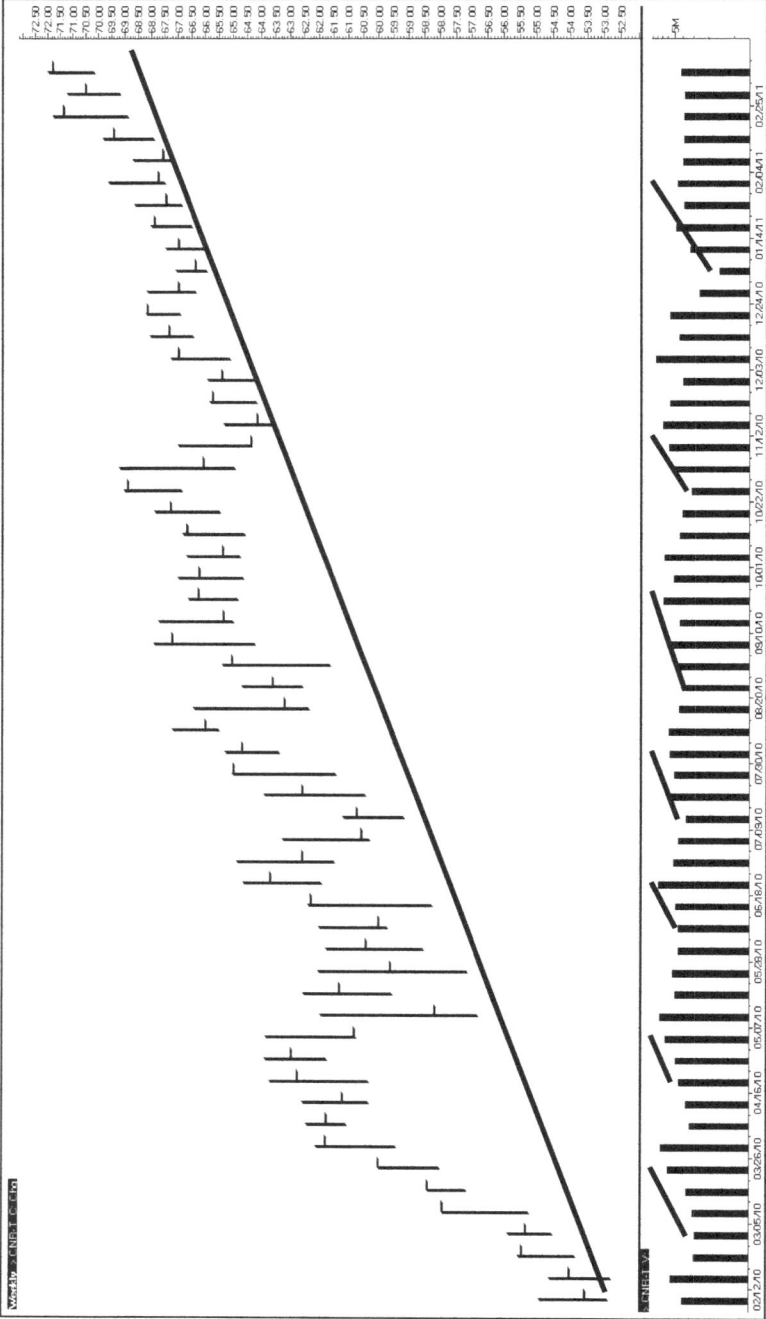

Figure 12. Chart of CN Rail in an uptrend with rising volume on the rallies. (Copyright © 1988-2008, Thomson Financial)

Sometimes a market will move within a trend that can be marked by both upper and lower trendlines connecting respectively successive peaks and troughs at the same angle. This phenomenon is known as a trend channel. It tends to add credibility to your identification of a strong trend.

The importance of volume

Volume is defined as the number of shares (or contracts, in the case of commodity futures) that trade in a given period.

On a stock's daily chart, each volume bar is located at the bottom of the chart below the given day's price. The volume bar represents the total number of shares that changed hands that day. Volume is important to investors and traders because it helps them verify the commitment and participation in the movement of the security price by the market players.

If volume expands as prices move in a trend, this is a good sign that the trend will continue. Expanding volume represents expanding participation in the security. The more shares (or contracts) being traded, the more excitement and interest is indicated surrounding the security's new trend. If more volume within a trend equates to more commitment by traders, it stands to reason that contracting volume implies the trend is in danger. I'll be mentioning volume and how to interpret it throughout this book. This is a good time to begin understanding its importance.

Expect volume in an uptrend to increase on market rallies and to ease off during pullbacks. This will give you evidence of a bull market. Weaker volumes, when prices decline, indicate lack of commitment by traders. The opposite should be true during a downtrend. Volume will increase on market troughs, indicating that the bears are in charge.

Within a downtrend, look for volume to contract during rallies. This indicates a lack of commitment to any positive price movement.

Within any major trend, look for lack of volume when a security rises or falls in price. This may be a signal that the trend will soon come to an end.

It's worth mentioning that securities do not rise or fall in price because there are more buyers (bulls) or sellers (bears) trading. There is always an equal number of buyers and sellers on the market. Clearly, for every buyer of a share there must be someone to sell that share to them. There are no one-sided trades. Securities rise in price when the buyers are more anxious to purchase the shares than the sellers are to sell them.

Sellers demand a higher price to sell their shares, and buyers are only too happy to pay that premium because of their bullish outlook. Logically, the reverse is true when securities fall in price. Then buyers are less anxious to step in, which pressures sellers to reduce their asking price in order to get out of their positions. The financial markets are ruled by supply and demand.

Sideways Markets

When markets or securities are stuck in a trading range, this is known as a sideways market. Rallies tend to reach a ceiling at about the same level as previous rallies. Declines tend to reach a floor at about the same price point as previous pullbacks.

The top of a trading range is known as support and the bottom of the range is considered resistance.

Support exists in a sideways market at prices where buyers are willing to pick the security up – they feel it's a bargain at that level. That's why the price tends to bounce off that level and not drop below it for too long.

Resistance in a sideways market, on the other hand, occurs when investors and traders want to sell the stock. They may have bought it at those levels before and simply want to sell it to get their money back. They may also feel the security has hit fair value at around that price level.

Securities trading in a sideways range have a hard time breaking out above their resistance levels or below their support levels. Typically, it takes a significant news event or dramatic change in investor attitude to break through support or resistance levels.

It's worth mentioning that markets spend most of their time in trading ranges and less time in up or down trends. You can see this by looking at figure 1 (page 2), which maps the Dow. Notice how markets spent a whole lot of time trading sideways – typically fifteen years at a time. Compare the sideways periods with the relatively fewer times spent in bull markets. This runs contrary to what many buy-and-hold investment managers would have you believe. They want to encourage you to invest your money in their products.

Moving Averages

Whether you're viewing an uptrend, downtrend, or trading range, the same rule always applies: the longer the security (or market) has been trading in that trend or range, the more likely it is to continue to move in that pattern or direction. You need to identify at least three successive rallies and troughs at similar price levels to confirm the existence of a sideways pattern.

If you're confused or unsure about the current direction of a market, there is a tool known as a moving average (MA) to help you to verify the existence of a trend. The moving average is the average price of a security over a given number of consecutive trading days immediately preceding the current trading day.

An MA is an important technical tool. It helps you identify and confirm the existence of a trend (up or down) or a sideways market. Moving averages smooth the price signal of a given security or market by filtering out the noise of day-to-day price swings. An MA represents a "composite photo of mass consensus," as Alex Elder puts it in his book *Trading for a Living*.

The classic moving average to help identify the longer-term trend is the 200-day MA. The 50-day MA helps you identify the shorter-term trend. Computer software and Internet sites conveniently calculate various types of moving averages for us. But it's useful to understand *how* they're calculated.

The simple 200-day MA, for example, is simply today's closing price for the security in question added to the prior 199 closing prices. Divide that figure by 200 and you have the current level of the 200-day MA. By calculating the 200-day MA every day, you are continuously discarding the data from 201 days ago and adding in today's new data. This means the MA line includes the current price movement of the security and still provides a record of its average price behavior over a longer period of time.

Some traders like to use an Exponential Moving Average (EMA) in place of the simple moving average described above. An EMA applies greater weight to the most recent prices, which means the price line will respond to changes more quickly.

Because the EMA is a more dynamic tool, it is especially useful for shorter-term trend changes.

On the other hand, simple MAs respond less vigorously to recent price changes. That's because they equally weight the data across the time span calculated. I recommend simple MAs for longer-term traders or those who want a less volatile trend indicator. You don't need to know how to calculate an EMA – it's rather complicated. Your favorite charting software or Internet charting service will do the heavy lifting for you.

Let's talk about the interpretation of MAs. If the security price remains above the simple 200-day MA, the long-term trend is considered to be up. If the security is also above the simple 50-day MA, then the evidence supports existence of a short-term trend. Many investors define a short-term trend as anything lasting fewer than six weeks. As described before, look for three higher highs and higher lows to identify an uptrend. In addition, look for the price to stay over the 50-day MA. If you are a long-term investor, look for the price to stay over the 200-day MA.

The slope of the moving average should be up for an uptrend and down for a downtrend.

Some investors prefer to see the shorter 50-day MA cross above the 200-day MA to confirm a new uptrend.

To confirm a new downtrend, they'll look for the 50-day MA to cross below the 200-day MA. From my perspective, this can be the sign of strength for the trend. However, it's not always necessary to observe a crossover before you enter (or exit) a position in the security. Waiting for a crossover often causes investors to miss out on a big part of the market's early upside movement.

If the security breaks the trendline you've drawn, check the moving average. It may just be changing its slope to a less aggressive line of ascent (or decline). However, if the security breaks down through its respective moving averages, this can be cause for concern. A stock formerly in an uptrend that breaks below its shorter 50-day MA is a less significant event than a break below its 200-day MA. Further, the crossing of the 50-day MA below the 200-day MA is another cause for concern. It may be the result of deeper fundamental problems with the security – especially if it's an individual stock.

We'll be reviewing on a deeper basis later in this book some other analytical tools for you to use in exploring the strength of the market. For now, realize that most things on the stock market happen for a reason. Check financial news sources for an unexpected negative earnings

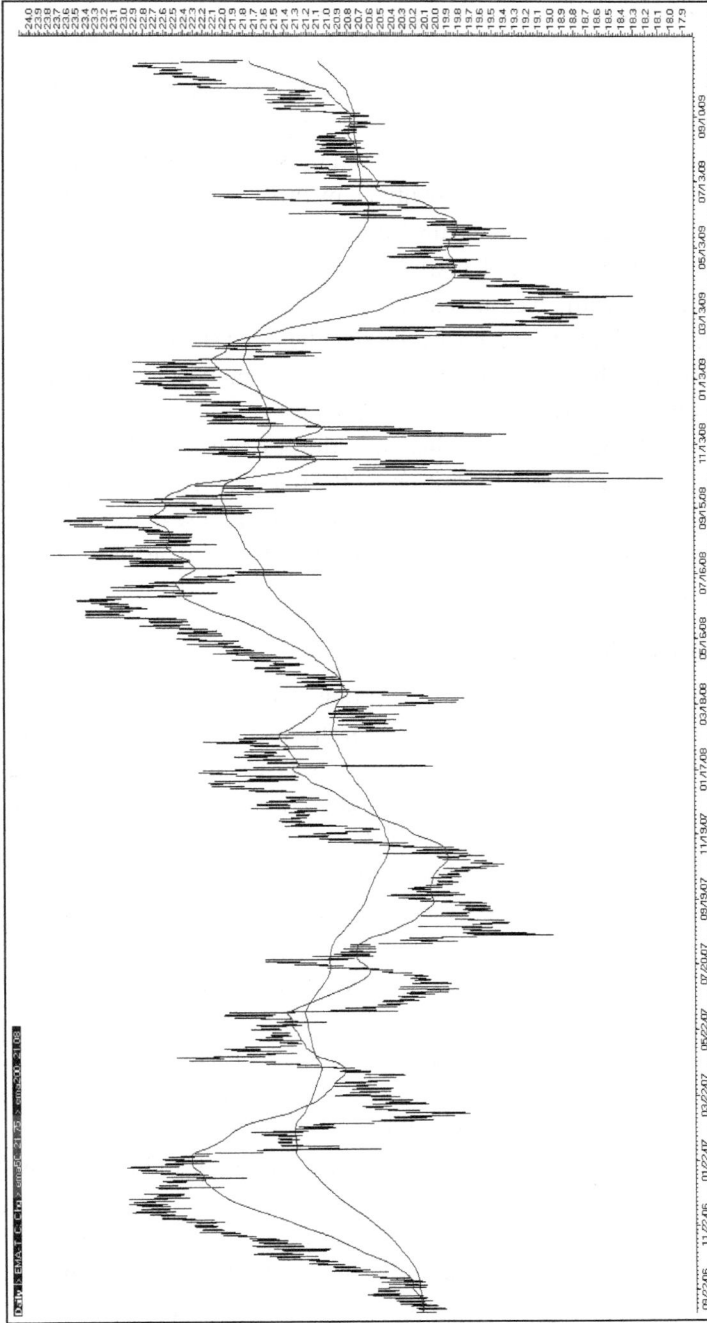

Figure 13. Chart of Emera with 50- and 200-day moving averages. Note that both MAs meandered through the chart during the sideways November 2005 to September 2009 period. As the stock began to trend upward that fall, the 200-day MA (thicker line) began to support the direction of the trend. The 50-day MA remained fairly whippy as the stock rallied and troughed violently in its new direction. (Copyright © 1988-2008 Thomson Financial)

TRENDS

report or negative forward guidance if you witness an MA confirmation of trend change.

As you now know, an uptrend in a market is more easily identified when you see three rising peaks and three rising troughs. In addition, you'll observe the security trading above an up-sloping moving average. Conversely, a downtrend can be identified by three declining peaks and troughs as the security trades below a down-sloping MA.

Sideways, or range-bound, markets move above and below their moving averages with no clear commitment to a trend. The moving average tends to look flat. There is no easily identified slope. Because of this, MAs tend to be less useful in confirming entry and exit points for a range-bound security. Rather, a flat MA tends to confirm that a trend does not exist for the security at this time. The best way to trade the security is to buy at or near the bottom of the trading range (support), and sell near the top of the range (resistance). The premise of this book is my belief that the markets have been, and will continue to be for the next few years, in very much of a range-bound pattern.

Point and Figure Charts

Let's end this chapter with a brief description of another trend identification tool, the point and figure chart, which is perhaps the purest form of trend charting. Some Technical Analysts use this form of charting exclusively for determining their entry and exit points. They adhere to the philosophy that you should stay invested in the security until the trend has ended. These technicians feel that the violation of a trendline, as described, is a less-than-perfect way of identifying the demise of a trend.

A point and figure chart offers the beauty of removing time from the X axis of the chart. (See figure 14, a P&F chart for the Russell 2000 Small Cap Index.) Instead, the chartist marks an X in a square located in a vertical column on a sheet of squared graph paper each time the security price moves up by a specified amount. Successive upward price movements result in a rising column.

The amount of price movement allowing you to mark an X in a box is called the box size.

A box size of $2 means the price of the security must move up by $2 on a given day in order to require adding an X to the top of the column.

Conversely, if the stock moves down by $2, a new vertical column is

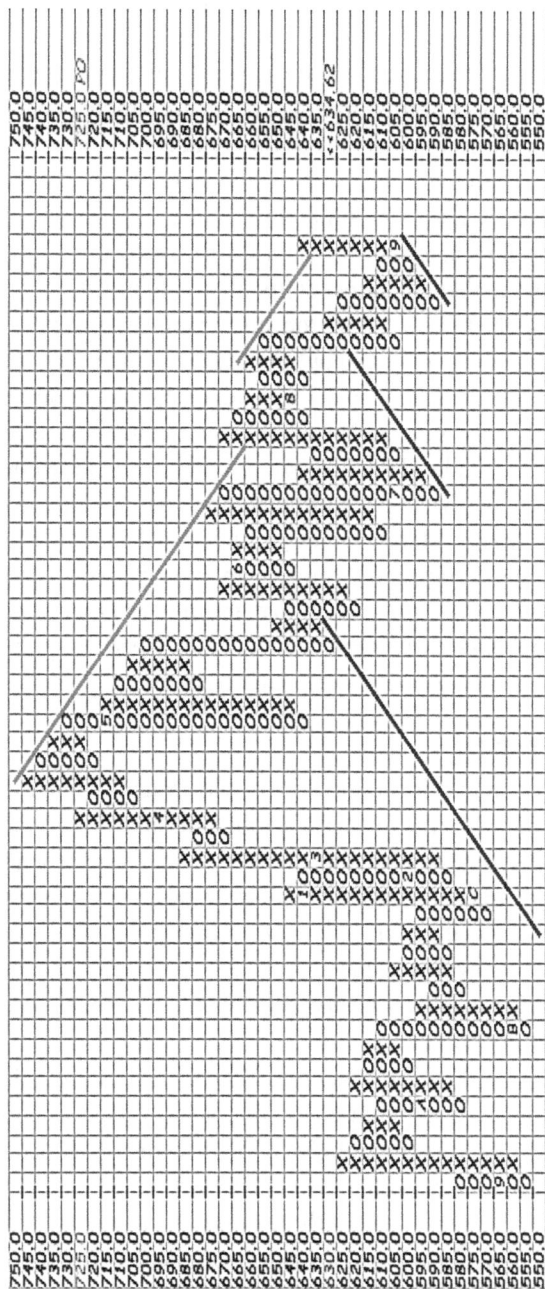

Figure 14. Point and figure chart of the Russell 2000 Small Cap Index from June 2010 to September 2010. The X column on the right indicates that this index has been moving up. Each box is $5 and the reversal criteria three points. This means the index must fall by $15 before a new downward O column is started. Note the breakout past the declining trendline. It suggests a potential continuation of the current rally or possibly a new trend. (Copyright © 2010, Thechartstore.com)

TRENDS

started and an O is placed in a square in that column below the level of a previous entry.

If prices do not change by the appropriate box size, no X or O is entered. The basics of this charting system are simple and logical. Stay long in the security as long as the trend is up. This is identified by an X column. When the trend reverses, and an O column appears, it's time to exit the security. There's no simpler form of trend identification available to investors. But there's always a catch, isn't there?

The most challenging aspect of point and figure charting is determining the box size. If it's too small, you'll experience frequent trend changes that force you in and out of the market at an unprofitable price. Conversely, if it's too large, you may end up staying in too long and lose your shirt. Ideally, an experienced point and figure chartist develops the knowledge to decide which box size should be used based on the characteristics of the security or market being followed and current market conditions. Many charting software packages offer point and figure charting with pre-determined box sizes. It's worth exploring this pure form of trend identification to determine whether it may aid you in your trading. Note that there are many other aspects of point and figure charting that are beyond the scope of this book.

In a Nutshell

This chapter on trends has shown you that securities move either up, down, or sideways. The formal way of identifying an uptrend or a downtrend is to draw a trendline that intersects three trough lows (for an uptrend) or three rally peaks (in a downtrend). We've also discussed how to compute a moving average line on your chart. Moving averages can provide further evidence that an uptrend is in place if the line stays below the current price of the security and is moving up (in an uptrend) or down (for a downtrend).

Sideways markets can be identified by their similarly priced peaks and troughs. You draw a horizontal line across the peaks and another horizontal line across the troughs to identify the top (resistance) and bottom (support) levels of a sideways market. To correctly identify such a market, you need to identify three peaks and three troughs with your horizontal lines. Throughout a sideways market, all but the shortest-term moving averages tend to meander sideways through the current price movement of the underlying security. If a security breaks out of a sideways pattern, you should watch for the development of a new trend developing in the direction of the breakout.

This chapter has also shown you the importance of using volume to confirm the commitment of traders to the existing trend. Volume should expand (i.e., increase) as the trend continues, particularly during the short-term peaks (in an uptrend) or rallies (in a downtrend). You will find many references to volume and its value in confirming the validity of the various chart formations in chapter 3.

You also learned about point and figure charting, which could be considered the cleanest way to focus on price direction and trend. Point and figure charts remove the variables of time and intraday pricing levels (high, low, and close) to focus exclusively on movement of closing prices.

3

FORMATIONS

Chart patterns and formations help us identify what stage or phase the market is in. They help pinpoint better entry points and selling points. They also help us identify whether the current trend is likely to continue, or whether it's coming to an end. It's worth becoming familiar with three basic types of patterns and formations: bottoming patterns, topping patterns, and continuation patterns.

As with all things in life, the financial markets never stay still. All trends come to an end or consolidate. At the very least, trends can be interrupted and form a temporary consolidation pattern that can last weeks or even months before returning to the trend again. Sideways markets also must eventually move out of their consolidating patterns and break into a new trend. The Buddha taught, some 2,500 years ago, that there is no such thing as permanence. All things change. Nothing stays the same. We suffer, he said, because of our resistance to change. The only way to stop suffering, according to Buddha, is to stop fighting change and accept it and adapt to it as a never-ending part of our existence.

This chapter shows you how to identify the patterns that signal continuation of a trend or the end of the current stage in the market. This ability will give you a leg up over other traders and investors who do indeed suffer by denying the impermanent nature of the financial markets. Use pattern recognition to correctly identify the market's current phase. Then adapt your trading strategies to suit the current climate. Don't fight the losing battle of ignorance and wishful thinking by hoping the current trend will continue indefinitely. Pattern recognition will enable you to buy and sell using natural changes on the markets.

We'll concentrate in this chapter on the patterns you should be most able to correctly identify during the various market phases. This book is intended to be a practical trading guide rather than a textbook, so I will not deal in this chapter with a some of the rarer or harder-to-identify formations and patterns.

Bottoming Patterns: Identifying Phase One in the Markets

Bottoming patterns are similar in numerous ways to topping patterns, which will be discussed shortly. Many of the patterns that create recognized bottom formations have mirror-image cousins in topping formations. For this reason, we'll spend a bit more time covering bottoming patterns. Once you grasp how to identify and trade during phase one bottom formations, you'll be able to apply the same logic to the identification and use of phase three topping formations.

Markets can and will change direction. Bottoming patterns, like topping patterns, are reversal formations. They signal that the direction of the market is changing from down to up. Reversal patterns form recognizable shapes that take days or weeks to complete. It's rare to see a security that was in a defined downtrend reverse direction one day immediately enter into a new uptrend. These occurrences (called V reversals for their shape) are too rare to be covered in this book.

Most reversal patterns leading into a sustainable new uptrend will take some time to build. The shift occurs as the struggle between the bulls and the bears begins to be won by one group or the other. In the case of a bottoming pattern, the bulls slowly become the dominant force on the market. They eventually drive the security price into a new uptrend.

I have chosen to focus on the five distinct formations you're most likely to encounter when searching for a security in phase one. These formations are head and shoulders, bottoms, rectangles, triangles, rounded bottoms, and double or triple bottoms.

Head and Shoulder Bottoms

The head and shoulders bottom is one of the easiest formations to identify and act on to initiate trades. It's one of the most common and reliable bottom patterns. For that reason, it's one of the most familiar patterns to traders in financial markets.

Unfortunately, this has led many individuals, armed with a little knowledge, to misinterpret or falsely identify this pattern on a regular basis. The Canadian Society of Technical Analysts (CSTA) offers a series of lectures to help students learn the material necessary for CMT accreditation. While I was attending these lectures, I befriended another student who was quite enthusiastic about technical analysis. Early in the program, before the real learning curve kicked in, this individual, like someone jumping at every shadow, tended to see a head and shoulders pattern on charts everywhere he looked. He was familiar with the pattern and always expected to find it. An experienced technician learns to overcome this tendency.

The head and shoulders pattern is characterized by its resemblance to the front profile of a person upside down. It contains at least one trough with high volume followed by a rally that forms the left shoulder.

After the left shoulder is formed comes another selloff trough. This time it brings the market to a lower price level than the left shoulder's trough. This second trough occurs with a somewhat lower amount of trading volume than the left shoulder selloff. This means we begin to see a lower commitment by investors and traders to the bear trend. The security price rallies to the approximate level of the rally that followed the left shoulder.

The security price now forms the head in this pattern. A third selloff brings the market down to a level that fails to go as low as that level achieved by the head. Again this happens on declining volume.

The security price rebounds for a third time to form the right shoulder.

A neckline can be drawn by connecting the rally tops of the two shoulders and head.

I don't enter a long position on a head and shoulder breakout unless there is a distinctive spike in volume upon the neckline breakout. You'll recall the importance of volume to verify the commitment and likelihood of follow-through upon a security's new direction. You can buy this security immediately upon breakout or wait for a near-term pullback to the neckline.

Pullbacks to the neckline occur frequently enough that it may be worth waiting in order to enter at this ideal price point. However, if you feel strongly about buying into the security, it may not be worth the risk of waiting for a pullback entry point that may never arrive. Once you have determined that a genuine breakout from a head and shoulders formation has occurred, you can enter the trade with a minimum objective for the price to move as the security moves into a phase two uptrend.

Estimate this minimum price objective by measuring the distance between the bottom of the head and the neckline. Suppose this measurement is $4. That means the breakout could reward investors with *at least* $4 in upside profits before moving into a phase three topping pattern.

You will find it is possible to estimate the minimum potential price movement objective upon a breakout by measuring from the deepest part of the chart formation. All reversal patterns exist because of a level of disagreement between the bulls and bears trading the market at that time. As prices swing up and down during the reversal formation, the actions of market participants show us how much variation in price (volatility) they're willing to tolerate. It's logical to project that, upon a breakout from a consolidation pattern (such as a bottom head and shoulders), the news or events that have inspired the breakout will contribute to an upside price movement mimicking the recent volatility of the security.

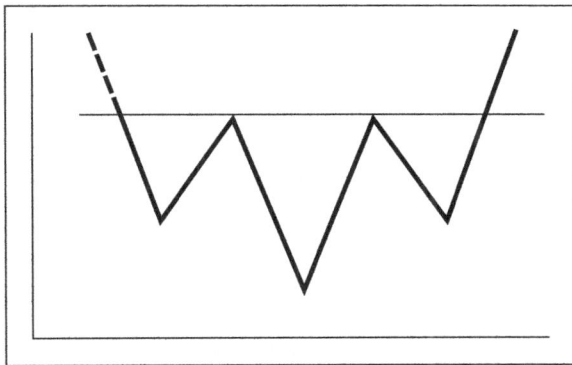

Figure 15. Head and shoulders bottom with neckline and upside projection.

There are a fair number of valid variations on the bottom head and shoulders pattern. For example, as often as not, you will see asymmetrical variations of the pattern. One shoulder may dip lower than the other.

Or you may observe two shoulders on one or both sides of the formation. The neckline may slope up or down. All of these variations are valid so long as the volume patterns remain consistent with the guidelines I've described. That is, you must observe gradually declining volume as the pattern progresses, followed by a considerable spike in volume upon a breakout. Further, the head must be lower than the shoulders no matter how many shoulders might exist.

The Three and Three Rule

The three and three rule states that, in order for a chart pattern to be considered viable, the stock must move by at least 3% over at least three days in the direction the chart pattern has predicted. When we look at most of the traditional patterns identified in technical analysis, there's usually a price level that the security must penetrate. For example, confirmation of a genuine head and shoulders breakout happens if and only if price penetrates the neckline by a minimum level of 3% for a period of three bars on your chart (three days on a daily bar chart).

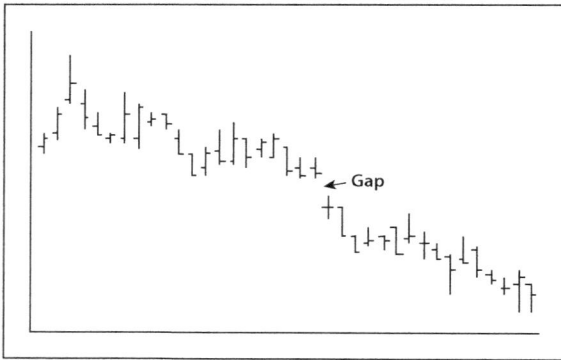

Gaps

Figure 16. Gap.

Gaps on a daily trading chart occur when a stock opens at a different price level than it closed at on the previous trading day. If there's no trading at the same price level between the close of one day and the opening price of the next, there's a gap or space on your bar chart. For example, if a security closes at $7.50 per share on day one and then opens the next trading day at $8.25, there's a gap or hole on the chart between $7.50 and $8.25. The gap represents the price zone in which the stock did not trade prior to opening at the higher level. A similar gap occurs if the stock closes at $7.50 and opens the following day at $6.00 per share. A gap appears on your chart between these prices.

Technical Analysts have identified and named many types of gaps. However, it's more important for investors to understand the implications of gaps than to identify and name them. Certain important implications of gaps should demand your attention.

Understand that gaps represent an exceptional level of fear or greed for the market. Imagine how excited traders must be about upside potential in the security of our previous example to buy the stock at $0.75 higher than it closed at the previous day. This is a 10% jump in the price with no stops between! Some exciting news or piece of information made its way into the minds of traders before the open of the new trading day. A gap represents a temporary period of emotional response to some new information by the investing public. This excitement is not likely to continue. The price move may be overdone.

I am a contrarian investor and tend to look at gaps as signals of massive investor sentiment. So I watch for a potential reversal in trend when the emotions of greed or fear begin to ramp down after the initial surge of excitement. For this reason, many gaps are filled at some later point as the security price action settles down and gives back some of the overdone upside (or downside) movement that caused the gap.

Rectangles

Because I've written this book to inspire you to invest differently in today's sideways market, it would be illogical if I didn't introduce the sideways or rectangular bottom reversal pattern.

Rectangles, unlike head and shoulders formations, always trade symmetrically. They're bounded by horizontal lines, one on top of the pattern and the other on the bottom. Prices remain range-bound and bounce up and down between these horizontal limitations. Occasional spikes above or below the horizontal lines may occur, but these are usually short-lived and infrequent. As with most price-reversal patterns, volume tends to contract as the pattern continues.

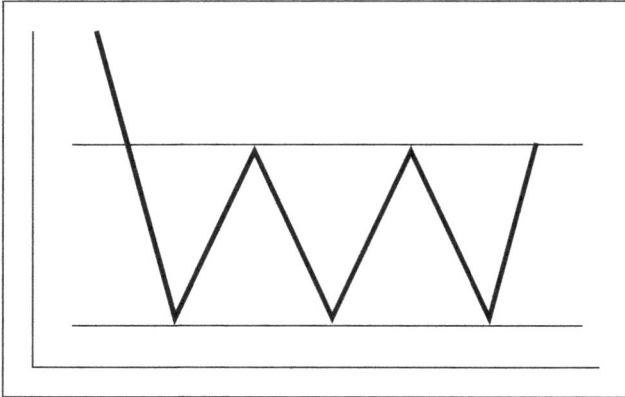

Figure 17. A market rectangle.

It's important to note that rectangles can break out to the upside or the downside. A downside breakout from a rectangle implies an impending bearish trend. Generally speaking, you should avoid buying the security while its price is within a rectangle pattern. The exception to this? Buy at or near the bottom and sell near the top of a deeper-than-normal rectangle. Look for a fairly sizable price difference between the top and bottom horizontal lines. A difference of less than 20% may not be worth trading.

In an upside breakout through the top (resistance) line of a rectangle, volume normally spikes. If it doesn't increase with the upside movement, you should be suspicious of a false breakout. Use the 3% and three-day rule to verify the validity of the breakout. Then decide whether to wait for a pullback to the former top of the trading range (top horizontal line) or whether to buy into the security right away.

The longer the rectangle has been in place, the greater the upside potential upon a valid breakout. Here price targets are not usually forecast by the depth of top to bottom maximum volatility. Instead, the upside minimum price target may be able to be estimated by measuring the width of the rectangle.

I'm not confident in the reliability of this method. It's true that the market hates inertia. It will display greater upside or downside volatility after a long period of consolidation within a given pattern. However, I think it's illogical to extrapolate the time the price action spends within a rectangular pattern into a meaningful price objective. But it may be true that a decisive breakout (on the upside or downside) from a long rectangle implies a fair amount of pent-up energy. A breakout may be enhanced as traders who previously sat on the sidelines are once again motivated by new potentials.

Symmetrical and Ascending Triangles

Triangles may occur in any of the four phases of the market. Owning a security during the formation of a triangle is dangerous. When the triangle forms after a long bear market, subsequently breaking out to the upside, you're probably seeing a phase one bottom reversal pattern. If it forms after a long bull market, subsequently breaking out to the downside, you're probably witnessing a phase three top reversal pattern. If it forms during a phase two bull market (uptrend) or phase four bear market (downtrend), subsequently breaking out in the same direction of the prior trend, it can be considered a continuation pattern.

Given these occurrences, the most important aspect of successfully trading a triangle formation is to *wait patiently until the direction of the breakout is established*. Don't hold a security or attempt to trade between the upper and lower boundaries during the formation of a triangle the way you would with a rectangle. As a triangle forms, prices move toward a tighter and tighter trading range. This makes the job of estimating entry and exit points within the formation very difficult. Furthermore, the direction of the breakout, whether up or down, should not be assumed.

Triangles come in three types. They are symmetrical, ascending, and descending. Bullish phase one triangles are limited to the symmetrical and ascending varieties. However, all three of these triangle types have some commonalities.

Triangles are composed of a series of price fluctuations that become tighter and smaller as the formation progresses. The formation looks exactly as the name implies. Picture a triangle lying on its side with its wide end at the left side of the chart and its sharp end at the right. Many traders, including me, refer to triangles as *coils*. This is because the price action is coiling, or getting tighter and tighter, as time progresses. As a triangle's trading range coils, it appears that traders are beginning to agree on a price.

As I've already mentioned, the market does not remain in inertia for too long. Impermanence is its very nature. Eventually, something happens to hasten a change in price action and create a breakout to the upside or downside of a triangle. As with other formations, that breakout usually occurs after a significant event or piece of news motivates traders to take action, aggressively acquiring (in the case of an upside breakout) or selling the security (downside breakout).

To identify a triangle, draw two trendlines to represent the upper and lower boundaries of the formation. Identify at least two rally tops before you draw the top boundary line. Identify at least two trough pullbacks before you draw the bottom boundary line.

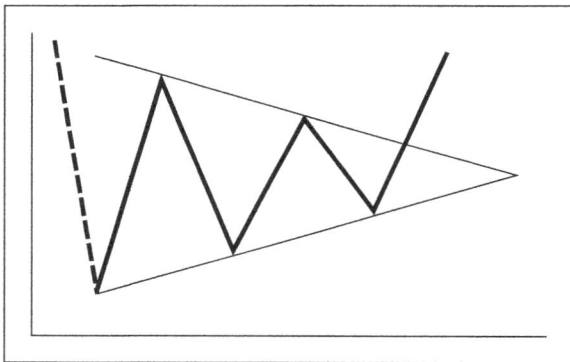

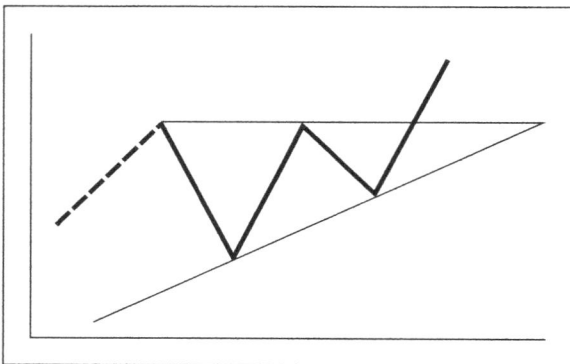

Figures 18 and 19. Symmetrical, ascending triangles with breakout and tests.

Symmetrical triangles are composed of price fluctuations that form top and troughs in a symmetrical fashion. The top line is down-sloping and the bottom line is up-sloping at a similar angle.

Ascending triangles differ from symmetrical triangles by having a horizontal upper boundary line that connects a series of roughly equally priced rally tops.

Triangles typically break out at about two-thirds to three-quarters of the way to the crossing point of the boundary lines. Volume tends to contract throughout the formation of the pattern. Volume should spike dramatically upon the breakout; low volume implies a potential false breakout.

As with most reversal patterns, you may often witness a final test of the breakout point when the price moves aggressively into a new trend. Once again, as a trader, you must make the decision whether to wait for the potential test or trade the breakout without waiting. As always, use the three and three rule to verify the validity of a breakout. The minimum price objective of a triangle breakout can be fairly accurately calculated.

Measure the left side (fattest end) of the triangle. Project that movement forward from the breakout point. Measuring the height of the left side of the triangle is really just measuring the maximum volatility that the security has recently experienced. It's reasonable to assume that the upside price movement from a bottom triangle breakout could equal its former range of price movement. So if the triangle measures a $7 move from peak to trough at its widest point, it may be expected that the stock will move up by at least $7 if a genuine upside breakout occurs.

Rounded Bottoms

Rounded bottoms are also known as "cup with handle" formations or "saucers." That's because they look like the bottom of a cup. The circular formation is followed by the common breakout point pullback test that reversal formations often display. It's the part of the formation resembling a handle on the right side of the cup.

A rounded bottom, like the rounded top, indicates a less violent trend than some of the formations mentioned before. This formation is a more gradual change in trend. Compare that with the series of volatile up and down price movements that eventually break a neckline or boundary line in other formations. The price swings making up the peaks and troughs

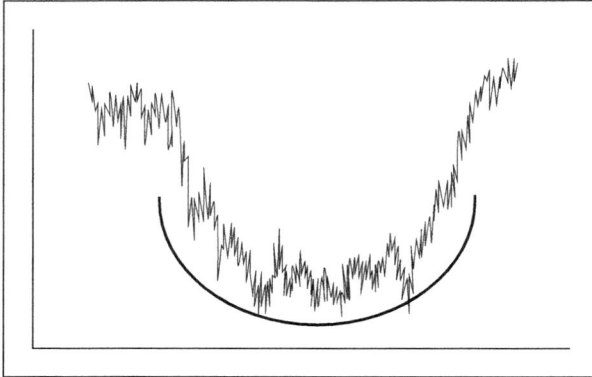

Figure 20. Illustration of a rounded bottom. (MetaStock)

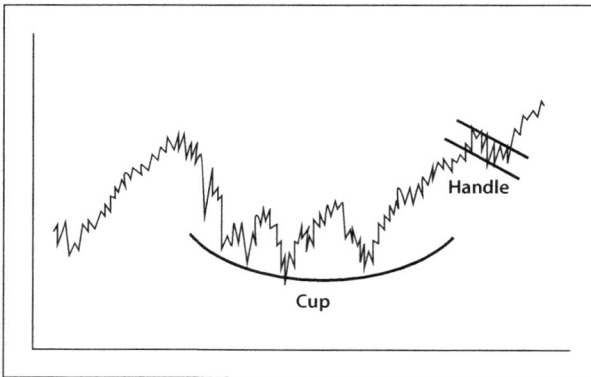

Figure 21. Cup and handle. (Kim Viney)

within this formation are, at most, the same size as they were during the phase four downtrend, if not smaller. The prior sharp angle of descent characterizing the phase four bear market subsides during the first half of this formation.

Sellers become less eager to dump their shares at the extreme price lows that have been reached.

Buyers are becoming more interested in the security and are ramping up their efforts to accumulate positions. As these gain in strength and conviction, the trend direction begins to shift up through higher highs and higher lows during the second half of the formation.

Because of the gentleness of this gradual shift in sentiment toward the market, the rounded bottom formation is one of the longer bottom patterns. It often takes several months to complete. There's usually no identifiable neckline or upper boundary line for you to draw. Instead, draw a rounded boundary line along the trough bottoms. Identification of the rounded appearance of the troughs is more important than a defined pattern for the rallies that make up this pattern.

The volume bars at the bottom of your chart will imitate the rounded price bars in this pattern. Volume is somewhat higher at the start of the formation, tapering off as selling pressure diminishes and the new uptrend tentatively takes hold. Again, volume must expand aggressively as the pattern finishes, showing that the bulls are firmly in charge of a new uptrend. A burst in volume and rising price activity signals the end of the rounded bottom formation and the beginning of a new phase two uptrend.

Use the three and three rule as confirmation of the breakout's validity. As noted before, a pullback (the "handle" to the "cup") may occur and provide a final entry opportunity. But you may not want to wait that long.

Double and Triple Bottoms

Double and triple bottoms are not as common as some of the other patterns discussed in this chapter. Despite their relative rarity, they are easily identifiable.

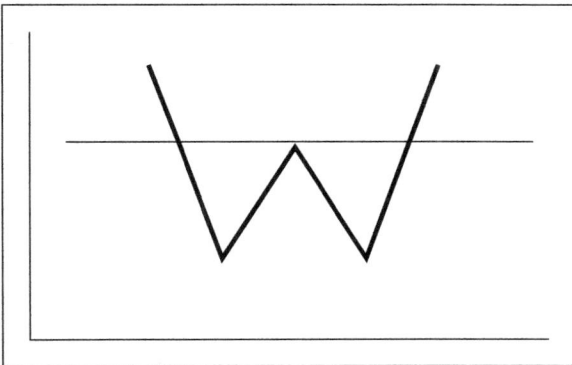

Figure 22. Double bottom with no neckline test.

Double bottoms are characterized by two trough low points. They are of relatively equal magnitude occurring after a phase four bear market trend.

Triple bottoms are characterized by (you guessed it) three troughs of similar magnitude.

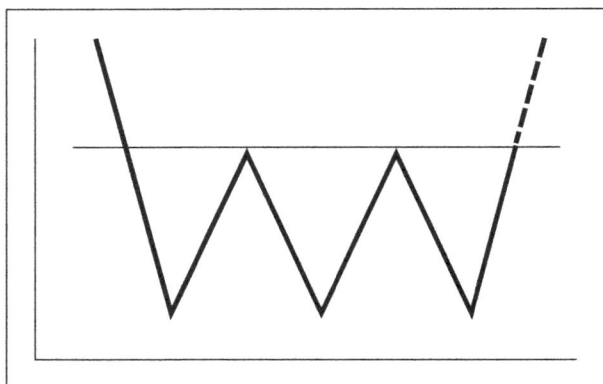

Figure 23. Triple bottom with no neckline test.

The low points of the troughs should land at a similar price point in order for you to classify the formation as true double or triple bottom formation. After each trough, price tends to rally back up to a horizontal neckline. A breakout past this neckline implies the end of the pattern and the beginning of a phase two bull market.

Be aware that head and shoulder bottoms are a more typical three-trough pattern than triple bottoms. Watch the price points of the troughs as confirmation of the pattern. One could actually call a triple bottom a rectangle, given our rule that a rectangle requires three successive peaks and troughs of equal magnitude. Technical analysts prefer to identify triple bottoms with a separate label. I've included them here in keeping with that tradition.

As with most reversal patterns we have seen, volume tends to be higher during the early stages of the formation. It contracts as the pattern progresses through each successive trough. Upon a breakout past the horizontal neckline, watch for a spike in volume. Use the three and three rule to confirm the legitimacy of the breakout. You read earlier about the traditional pullback in prices testing the neckline. This often occurs upon a breakout from head and shoulders, rectangles, and rounded bottoms. You won't likely see this on a double or triple bottom.

Topping Patterns: Identifying Phase Three in the Markets

You'll find a variety of topping patterns in phase three on the markets. These are your signals to get out of a security or market before a shift into a phase four bear market ensues. Many patterns occurring in phase three are merely bottoming patterns that have been flipped upside down. These patterns include head and shoulders tops, rounded tops, double tops, triple tops, and triangles. All of these upside-down patterns display similar volume characteristics to their bottoming pattern counterparts. That includes neckline tests where applicable.

Apply the same rules used to identify bottoming formations to identify these topping patterns. Here you apply them to the identification of the characteristics of rising and falling peaks rather than rising and falling troughs as with bottom patterns. For example, to identify a head and shoulders top, look for three peaks with the highest one being in the middle (as opposed to three troughs with the lowest in the middle as seen in a head and shoulders bottom).

As the head and shoulders top develops, watch for volume to contract on each successive peak, just as it does on each successive bottom in the bottom version of this pattern. Draw a neckline at the pullback point after each peak. Be aware that the formation may occur on an angle with a slanted neckline. Similar to bottom head and shoulder patterns, topping head and shoulder patterns can display more than one shoulder on one or both sides of the head. Look for a spike in volume upon a downside breach of the neckline.

Finally, you may often see a test or rally back to the neckline after a breakout. As you can see, interpreting one of these topping formations is logical and easy to do once you've mastered the bottom version.

You will find that rectangles are rarely topping patterns. They tend to be bottom or continuation formations. If you see a rectangular pattern occurring during a bull market, it's not likely a sign of an impending end to the phase two uptrend. Watch for a breakout through the upper boundary line of resistance to confirm the continuation of the bull market. Patterns that are unique to phase three topping formations include broadening tops and diamond tops. As with bottoming patterns, I have deliberately left out some of the harder-to-identify topping patterns such as rising wedges and various bearish candlestick patterns.

FORMATIONS

47

Descending Triangles

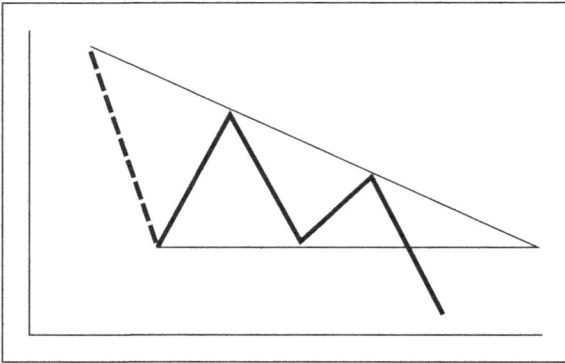

Figure 24. A descending triangle with breakout.

Descending triangles differ from symmetrical triangles. The bottom boundary line is drawn horizontally rather than on a rising angle. This is because the troughs of the various price fluctuations in the formation are reaching roughly equal price points. They create a flat base. You trade descending triangles like you trade one of the bullish triangle patterns. Wait for a breakout through the lower support line. Then use the three and three rule to verify its validity.

Broadening Tops

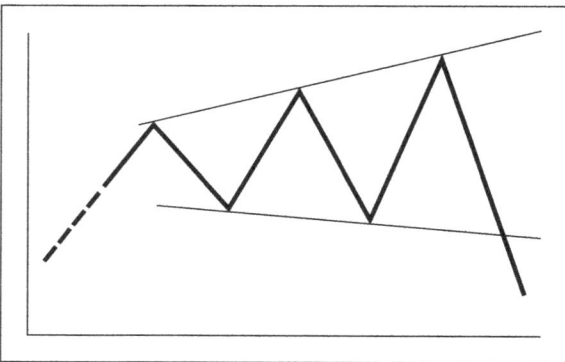

Figure 25. A broadening top with breakout.

A broadening top looks like a triangle formation that has been flipped around to face the opposite way. Fluctuations with narrow peak-to-trough movements start on the left side of the chart and become wider as the pattern continues. Volatility increases as the bulls and bears become less certain where the market is going.

Draw boundary lines along the widening peaks and troughs. Look for at least two successively rising peaks and two successively declining troughs to confirm the pattern, the opposite of what you find in a triangle. Then draw your trendlines. Unlike a triangle, which can break out in either direction, broadening formations virtually never break out to the upside. As in most reverse patterns, volume tends to contract as the pattern develops. The exceptions are rounded tops and bottoms which display rounded volume patterns.

When the security penetrates the lower trendline, watch for a volume surge. Use the three and three rule to confirm the movement. The security moves into a phase four bear market at this point.

Diamond Tops

Diamond tops are the next logical formation after broadening tops. The essence of a diamond top formation is that it's a broadening top up to the central part of the formation followed by a traditional triangle in the latter right side of the formation. Together, they form a diamond pattern.

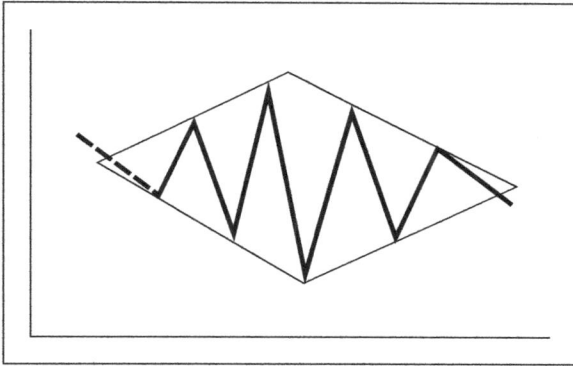

Figure 26. Cap A diamond pattern.

This formation is largely seen in phase three tops. Theoretically, an upside breakout from a diamond formation is a bullish sign. I have never witnessed such a phenomenon, however.

Diamond tops are rare but fairly easy to identify. The diamond pattern occurs over a shorter term than triangle or broadening formations. It must be identified early if you're to have time to react to its (usually) bearish implications. Volume will tend to contract through the pattern and spike upon a breakout. Neckline pullbacks or tests are not common. Prepare to pull the sell trigger quickly if you feel that you have identified a likely diamond top.

Continuation Patterns: Confirmation of Phase Two and Phase Four Trends

Rectangles and triangles have been classified in this chapter as reversal patterns. You've learned to identify and confirm the validity of a breakout from their upper or lower boundary lines by using volume and the three and three rule.

Rectangles and triangles can also be identified as continuation patterns. Continuation patterns may be considered as pauses or consolidation formations within the greater context of a trending market. You can identify continuation patterns by observing the direction of their breakouts from these periods of consolidation relative to the preceding trend.

For example, a triangle breaking out of its upper boundary line in a phase four bear trend can be identified as a phase one basing formation. Conversely, an upside breakout from a triangle during an existing phase two bull market is a sign that the bullish trend continues.

Triangles and rectangles can be reversal patterns or continuation patterns. Flag and pennant patterns are strictly continuation patterns. These patterns occur only in phase two bull markets or phase four bear markets. They are short term in length when compared with rectangles and triangles.

I've personally observed that flags and pennants occur more often during uptrends than downtrends. This doesn't imply that you won't ever see them during a downtrend. Perhaps they are rarer then because downtrends are usually shorter in length and sharper in angle than uptrends. Traders and investors sell positions much more rapidly than they accumulate them. This leaves less time for the market to momentarily consolidate and form these short-term patterns.

In any case, watch for flags and pennants to occur during a bull or bear market as verification that the trend will continue. They point to potential entry and exit points within a fast-moving market. You'll usually see a series of them somewhat randomly distributed within a trending market. Don't worry about confirming these ultra-short formations with the three and three rule or volume verification.

Flags and Pennants

Flags and pennants can be seen during either an uptrend (phase two) or a downtrend (phase four).

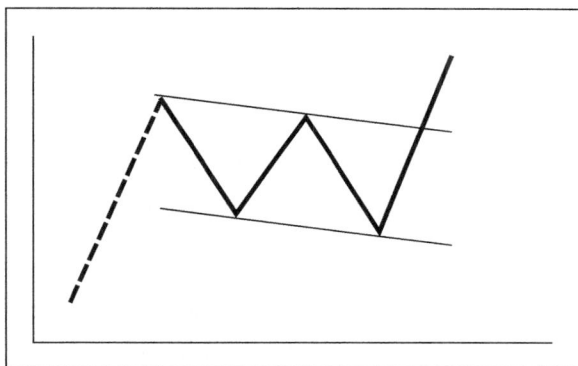

Figure 27. Flag.

A flag looks like a very short rectangle that is usually trading at a declining or ascending angle. During an uptrend, a flag slopes down from the pressure of traders and investors taking profits on its rapidly advancing position. During a downtrend, a flag slopes up to the right as some traders and investors, convinced that the security has become a good value, accumulate shares.

In either case, there is a decline in volume through the creation of the formation. Volume decline indicates that this short and small reversal against the trend represents a minority vote within the greater population of traders and investors who are following the security. On occasion, a flag may trade sideways in a way that looks like a small rectangle. More often than not they tend to slope down.

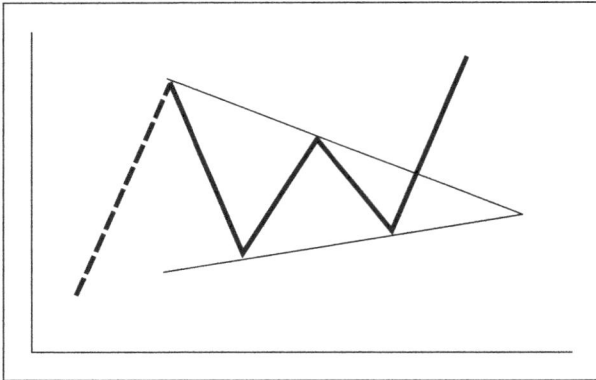

Figure 28. Pennant.

Pennants appear as very small and narrow triangle. Like a flag formation, pennants usually slope against the prevailing trend. During uptrends, a pennant will tend to slope down. During a downtrend, a pennant usually slopes up.

As with flags, volume tends to decline as the formation develops. Also as with flags, pennant formations represent a minority of investors or traders who have decided to trade against the trend. This is evidenced by the declining volume pattern. You may see the occasional symmetrical pennant without a slope. That is the exception rather than the rule. Trade in the direction of the major trend as you would with a flag if you witness the formation of a pennant.

In a Nutshell

This chapter has covered a number of the more prominent patterns and formations that you'll see on price charts. By learning these patterns, you will be able to identify the current phase of the market. This will enable you to correctly time your entry and exit strategy within that phase.

Phase one, the basing phase, is typically made up of consolidation patterns such as the head and shoulders bottom, rounded bottoms, double and triple bottoms, rectangles, or triangles. Upside breakouts occur through their horizontal resistance levels.

Phase three, the topping phase, can be identified by the inverse cousins of the consolidation patterns seen in phase one. Upside-down versions of these patterns create head and shoulders tops, rounded tops,

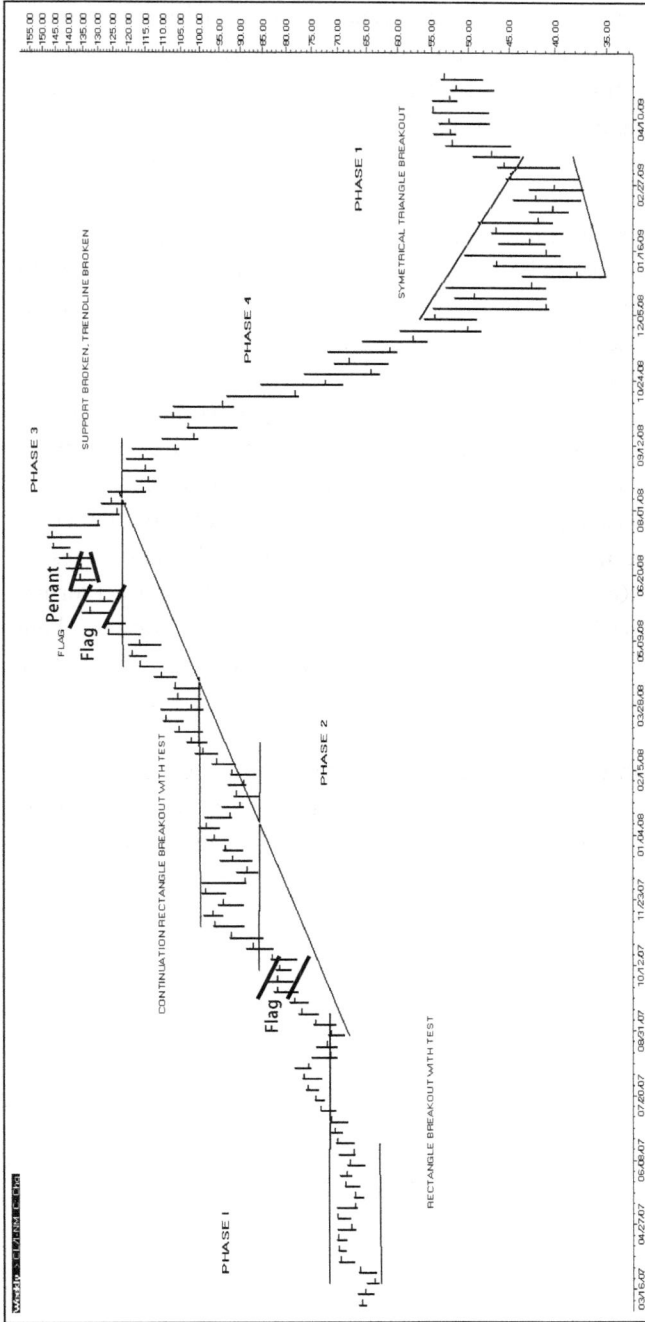

Figure 29. Spot oil chart, March 2007 to March 2009. Note the phase one rectangle breakout and successful testing of the breakout point. The market enters phase two by the middle of 2007. It is punctuated by various flags and pennants, including one large continuation rectangle pattern until the middle of 2008. In July 2008, the market changes direction as a neckline support area *and* the bullish trendline are both violated at around $125 per barrel. Oil prices decline aggressively until early 2009. Then a symmetrical triangle begins to form. Sharp-eyed traders wait for an upside breakout on the triangle before committing to the new phase two bull market. (Copyright © 1988-2008 Thomson Financial)

FORMATIONS

53

double and triple tops, and of course rectangles or triangles. Downside breakouts occur through their downside support levels. The menu of potential phase three patterns contains a few other formations that are uniquely topping patterns. For instance, diamonds and broadening formations occasionally show up on a chart to signal the end of a phase two uptrend.

I decided to exclude one topping pattern, the rising wedge, from this chapter's discussion because it is so difficult for novice technicians to identify it. It's also relatively rare. At this point, you're better off if you can identify and trade a few usable patterns rather than taking chances on patterns you don't fully grasp.

Phases two and four are trending phases. The patterns we see within them are known as continuation patterns. These patterns are both smaller in magnitude and shorter in duration. The most common continuation patterns are flags and pennants. Triangles and rectangles, typically seen in the phase one and three reversal stages of a market, also sometimes occur within a trending market. For example, suppose the market forms a triangle after having been trending for some time. Watch for a breakout in the direction of the prior trend. This signals real conviction by traders leading into a likely continuation of that trend for an extended period of time to come.

Chapters 1 through 3 focused on identifying the current phase of the market and providing the most important tools for trading effectively within that phase. The next chapter delivers some specific tools to refine your entry and exit timing.

4

MOMENTUM

THIS chapter shows you a practical way to use momentum indicators to refine the entry and exit points of the formations and trends you've learned to identify in previous chapters. Momentum oscillators are another important tool to help ensure the proper timing of your investment decisions.

How Momentum Indicators Work

If you and a friend were to toss a baseball back and forth, you would notice that the ball increases its height shortly after it leaves your hand. It then reaches a point where that height begins to decline as it gets closer to its objective. Just after the point of maximum height, the ball will begin to curve downward as it heads toward your friend's glove. Technicians call the point of maximum height on a security chart *overbought* because the speed and direction of the security price are soon to change to the downside. Conversely, when the depth of the security price is at maximum, it's considered *oversold*. Oversold securities bounce up like a basketball that has been aggressively thrown against the floor.

Momentum analysis backs up the trend, formation, and volume

analysis you've been learning in this book. By understanding how to interpret momentum indicators, you can finesse your entry point. Obviously, you want to avoid buying a security if it is temporarily overbought and ready to start curving down, like our baseball. Conversely, you may want to expedite entry into a position if the security has been oversold. It may be ready to bounce up, as in our basketball example.

Momentum oscillators identify extremes in the movements of securities. If a momentum indicator reads as overbought, this suggests that traders and investors have become overly optimistic. As the late, great Sir John Templeton put it, "To buy when others are despondently selling and to sell when others are greedily buying requires the greatest fortitude and pays the greatest reward." We want to buy when others are despondently selling and sell when others are greedily buying.

Momentum oscillators help us bet against the crowd's fear and greed. They show us when traders and investors have gone too far overboard in fearfully selling or overzealously buying. Extremes shown by a momentum indicator show that the market may be about to change direction.

These oscillators often signal oversold and overbought readings throughout phase one bottom formations and phase three topping formations. The market swings up and down between overbought and oversold while the bulls and bears wrestle for control. Momentum indicators also signal overbought sell readings at the end of a phase two bull market when securities have advanced too aggressively. They give oversold buy readings at the end of a phase four bear market when traders have sold securities off despondently.

Momentum oscillators sometimes trend in the opposite direction of a security when a security is in a phase two bull market or phase four bear market. *Divergence* is the term for when a momentum oscillator displays a directional price trend that is not the same as the price trend of the security chart it is tracking (e.g., one is going up while the other is going down). Momentum divergences are important indications of an impending change in trend direction for a security. If a momentum indicator is trending in the opposite direction of the security you're watching, expect the security to change direction soon.

There are many momentum indicators to apply to securities analysis. Given my desire to keep this book as pragmatic as possible, I'm going to focus on the easiest to use and easiest to interpret momentum indicators.

I will begin this chapter by explaining the simplest of all momentum indicators, the Rate of Change (ROC) oscillator. Then I will discuss two other popular indicators suitable for most investors and mid-term traders. These include my personal favorite, the Relative Strength Indicator (RSI), and the very popular Moving Average Convergence Divergence indicator (MACD).

Many momentum indicators are available through popular technical analysis software programs. Some of these indicators are beyond the scope of this book. For example, Stochastics, and Williams %R are fast-moving indicators often used by sophisticated Technical Analysts and traders. Other oscillators combining momentum with trading volume have been designed by the greatest minds in technical analysis. I encourage you to read *Martin Pring on Market Momentum* if you wish to learn more about this fascinating area.

Using Momentum Indicators

There are two main ways to interpret and apply any momentum indicator. The first is to identify *extreme levels* on the indicator (overbought and oversold). The second is to confirm the *trend* of the indicator (divergence) to see if it matches the trend of its underlying security. Let's take a look at both of these.

Overbought and Oversold

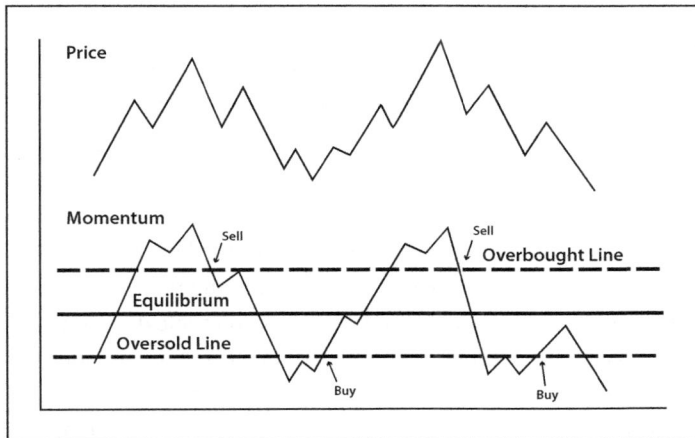

Figure 30. Illustrations of market when overbought and oversold.

Momentum indicators are oscillators that are usually plotted in a separate window on your chart. These indicators oscillate above and below an equilibrium center line. The purpose of plotting a momentum oscillator is to determine whether the crowd has become overzealous in buying or overly pessimistic in selling. When investors and traders run the market up to an unsustainably high level, the market is considered overbought. If it has sold off too quickly and aggressively, it is considered oversold. Momentum indicators help identify more precisely when a security reaches an overbought or oversold level.

Some indicators, like the Rate of Change indicator discussed below, do not have contained boundaries within which they are confined. Other indicators, such as the Relative Strength Indicator, are contained within defined horizontal zones.

In either case, you choose both the upper and lower levels for your chosen oscillator to reach before the security in question begins to change direction. The software program that plots the momentum oscillator usually allows the input of your own horizontal lines representing the upper overbought and lower oversold extremes. Position these lines so the space between them contains most of the trading activity of the security. The position of these horizontal lines should coincide with the significant price peaks and troughs the security has experienced.

You now have an indicator that shows when the odds of a top (top horizontal line) or of a bottom (lower horizontal line) increase. The longer the time frame plotted by the oscillator, the more significant the overbought or oversold readings become.

You will learn more about plotting various momentum time frames in this chapter. For now, it is key for you to understand two things.

First, when a momentum indicator breaches the top horizontal line, the security is considered overbought. Avoid it for new purchases. If you own it, consider selling.

Second, when the momentum indicator breaches the lower horizontal line, the security is considered oversold. Consider buying it.

Momentum indicators should not to be used as your sole decision-making tool. Consider an overbought or oversold reading in a broader context. Think about what phase the market is in. Analyze trends or formations within that phase. For example, consider a solitary oversold reading by a momentum oscillator. This is not enough data to base a trading decision on. Alone, the momentum oscillator may signal an insignificant price rally that isn't worth trading. Instead, proceed as follows. First, identify the phase of the market. Then determine its current trend or formation. Only after these steps should you refine your decisions by interpreting the momentum oscillator.

Divergence

When a security trends up (phase two) or trends down (phase four) you normally see the trend of a momentum indicator following along. If its trend does not match that of the underlying security, this is known as divergence. It is a strong indication that the trend is about to end.

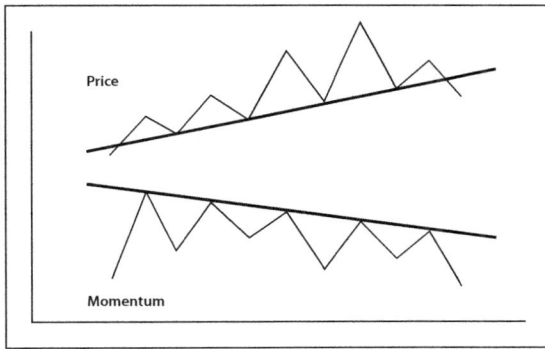

Figure 31. Up/down divergences.

Divergence in trend between the underlying security and a momentum oscillator suggests the security's trend is beginning to accelerate or decelerate. For example, the momentum indicator trends up while the security has been in a phase four downtrend. This may be a sign that the downtrend will end soon and the security will be moving into the phase one basing period.

Similarly, sometimes you see the momentum indicator make a higher low than its last trough. Meanwhile, the security went on to make a lower low in its downtrend.

When the security price falls to a new low while the oscillator does not, this is considered a bullish divergence. It is a sign of a potential positive change in trend for the security. Likewise, a new high on a security during an uptrend not confirmed by a new high on its oscillator is usually a bearish indicator.

Oscillators that diverge to trend up or down during a phase one top or phase three reversal pattern can indicate an imminent completion and breakout of their respective patterns. Consider a rising momentum oscillator during a phase one rectangular basing pattern. It might indicate the arrival of an upside breakout from the rectangle very soon, then a transition into a phase two bullish trend. I've included illustrations of a momentum indicator with a negative divergence and one with a positive divergence against an underlying security in figure 32 below.

The Simple Rate of Change Oscillator

The Rate of Change (ROC) indicator is the easiest momentum oscillator to construct and understand. Simply compare today's price with the price of the security in a given earlier period. For example, calculate a ten-day ROC by comparing today's price with the price from ten days ago. Most technical analysis software programs label the ROC oscillator as "the momentum indicator." This is a bit misleading because it suggests that ROC is the only momentum indicator out there. That is not the case.

The ROC formula is calculated as follows: ROC = P / Pn

P is the latest closing price. Pn is the price from a number of days ago, (ten days ago in the case of a ten-day ROC).

If the latest closing price is the same as it was ten days ago in a ten-day ROC, the oscillator does not move on your chart. If the latest price is greater than it was ten days ago, it is plotted as a positive move. If P is below the price of ten days ago, it's plotted as a negative move. The ROC formula is presented here to support your understanding of how the indicator works. Your computer software program will do the actual calculations. Your job lies in the interpretation and application of its data.

When you choose the time span for the ROC indicator, or any other momentum oscillator for that matter, it is important to choose the time span that provides the best entry and exit points in the past. Base it on your preferred trading horizon for that security. You never find the perfect time span for the ROC indicator because markets are in constant flux. Instead, you look to find the time span that works well most of the time for the majority of the securities and markets that concern you.

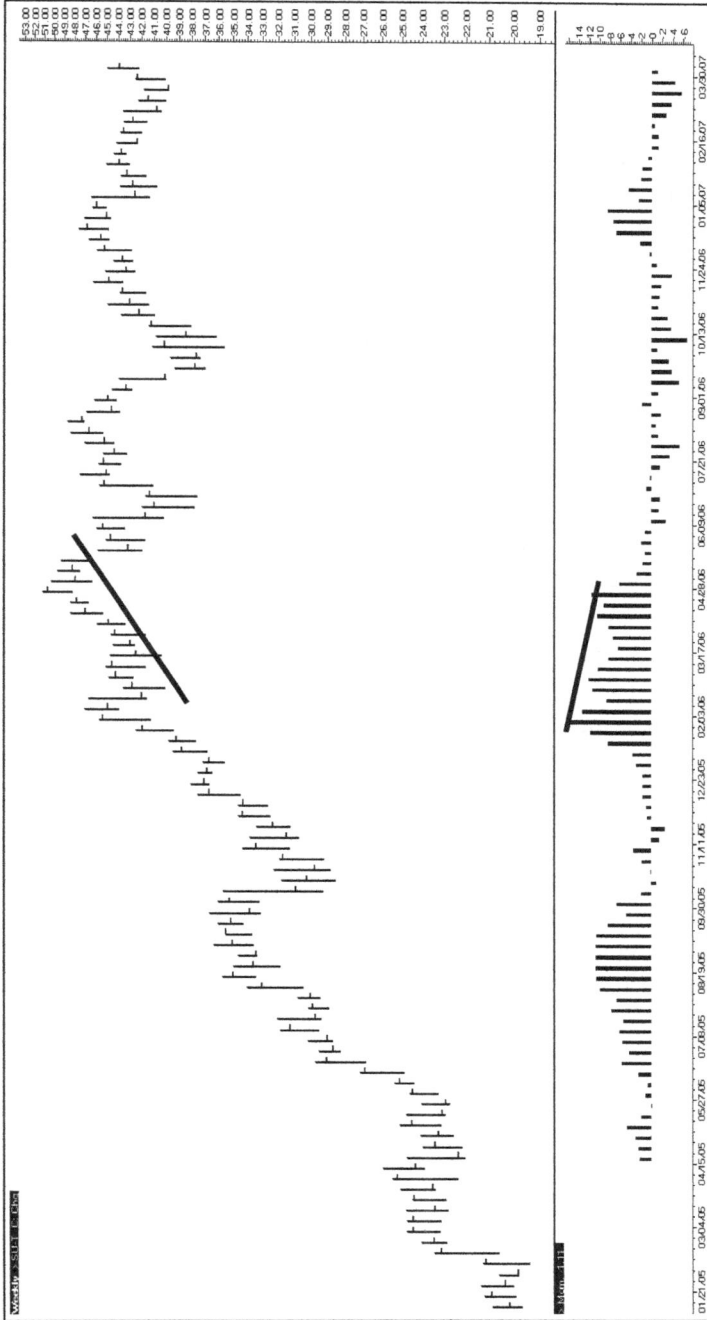

Figure 32. Suncor January to November 2005 to March 2007. The Rate of Change momentum indicator is shown here as a histogram at the bottom of the chart. It makes lower highs as the stock makes higher highs between January and April 2006. This divergence between the stock and the ROC gives us a clue as to Suncor's decline from $50 per share to $42 per share over the following 11 months. (Copyright © 1988–2008 Thomson Financial)

MOMENTUM

Many traders and investors seem to favor an ROC with a comparison span of nine to twelve days. You need to try various time spans in the ROC indicator to see which provides the best entry and exit signals for the market in which you trade.

Let's briefly cover how to choose horizontal overbought and oversold zones. Use the crosshair tool on your charting software to identify ideal historical entry and exit points on the security. Next, move the horizontal zone lines to levels that line up with those historic turnaround points. Arrange the horizontal lines in a position where they would have been breached during major market troughs and peaks in the past. They need to be positioned to eliminate the majority of the less important market noise. Choosing the ideal time span and horizontal zones on the ROC oscillator takes a bit of time. It also takes a bit of guesswork before you find the ones that work best for you in the market environment you are experiencing at the time.

The Relative Strength Index

The Relative Strength Index is more commonly known as the RSI oscillator. It should not be confused with another common technical tool known as the Comparative Relative Strength (CRS). RSI is a momentum indicator. CRS is a comparison of one security's strength to another.

RSI was created by Welles Wilder. It was originally introduced in his 1978 book *New Concepts in Technical Trading*. Most Technical Analysts, including me, feel RSI is a superior momentum oscillator compared with the basic ROC indicator discussed above.

This indicator is readily available and calculated for you on virtually any software or Internet charting service. There's no need to bother with presenting the formula on these pages. Basically, RSI calculates the average of the close prices for your selected security on the up days over a period of time. Next, it calculates the average of the close prices on the down days for the same period. These two averages are compared by dividing the up-day average by the down-day average.

Wilder originally suggests that a 14-day time span be used to calculate RSI. As with other indicators, it is worth experimenting with different values. The result of the above division is divided into 100 and then reduced by 100 to fit within a confined price scale. Each day the

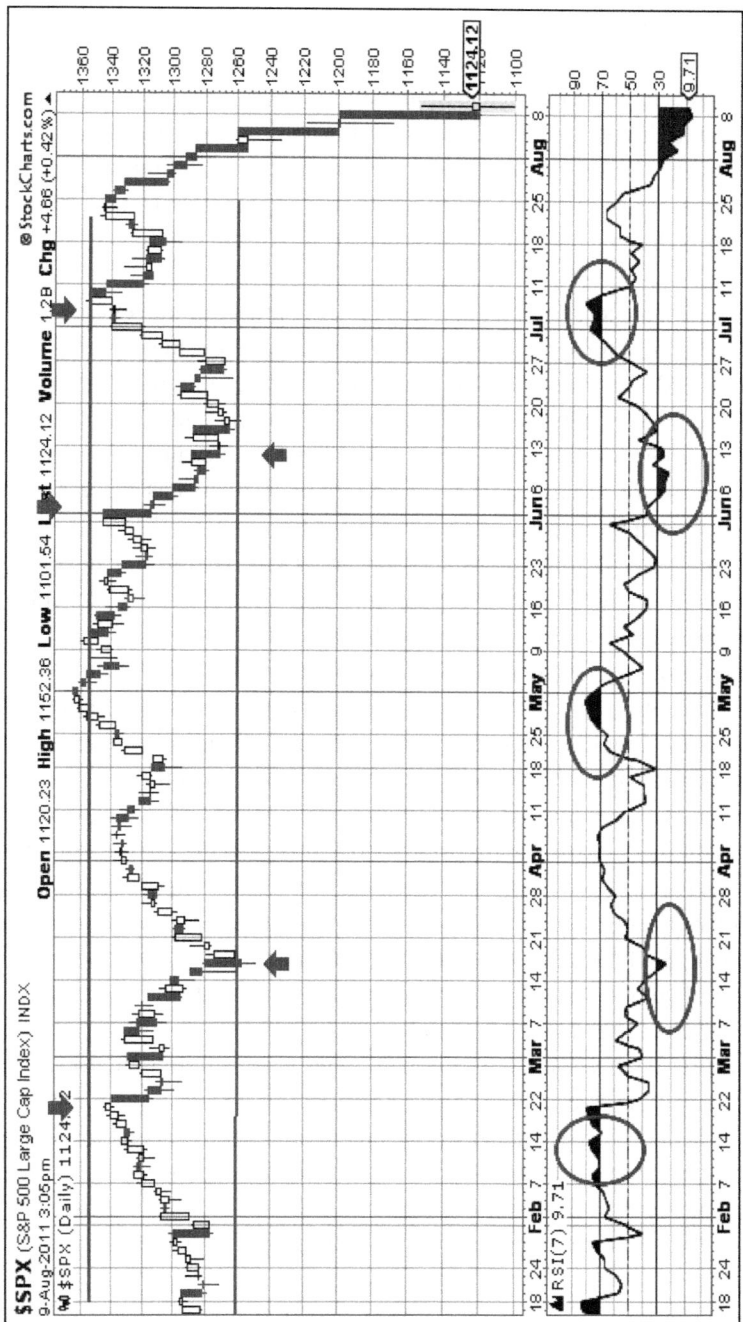

Figure 33. It's almost too easy. The chart of the S+P 500 during the spring and summer of 2011 illustrates the use of RSI in locating key overbought (sell) and oversold (buy) points.

MOMENTUM

result is calculated and the most recent data are added to the plot on your chart while the oldest data are dropped.

RSI tends to be a more stable momentum indicator than ROC. That's due to the averaging of the up and down days. The longer the time span chosen for the calculation, the shallower the RSI indicator's movements. It also offers the advantage of having a universal standard scale versus the varying scales that occur when plotting the ROC indicator.

RSI's absolute levels are set at 0 and 100. The indicator moves are contained within those extremes. Wilder found that by using a 14-day time span RSI, the majority of movements of the oscillator land between 30 and 70. A reading below 30 by RSI suggests that the underlying security has become oversold. It may be due for a bounce up. A movement above 70 suggests that the underlying security has become overbought and is due for some level of correction.

You may choose a different span than the 14-day default time in your computer software. If you do, keep in mind that the 30/70 levels probably need to be reduced to capture more of the indicator's extremes.

As I did with the ROC indicator, I recommend identifying the major peaks and troughs that the underlying security experiences. Then note the corresponding RSI levels in order to optimize where you place the horizontal extremes. Shorter-term traders may want to capture and subsequently sell on more frequent market movements. They may wish to experiment by reducing the RSI time span and/or moving the horizontal extremes. If you choose to deviate from the 14-day RSI default settings in your software program, be sure to manually back test the effectiveness of your changes. Then adjust them appropriately by running the crosshair function of your software along the peaks and troughs of your security to optimize your variations.

Interpret RSI the same way as you do other momentum oscillators. Look for readings above 70 to trigger potential sell signals. Look for readings below 30 to trigger a possible buying opportunity. Look for divergences in the directional trend of RSI versus the trend in the underlying security. Determine if conflicting new lows or new highs between RSI and the underlying security are another form of divergence.

The Moving Average Convergence Divergence Indicator

In chapter 2, you learned how moving averages smooth out the daily ripples and short-term price movements. That helps you identify the major trend of an underlying security. The Moving Average Convergence Divergence indicator (MACD) is unique. Rather than using MAs to verify trends, it uses three Exponential Moving Averages (EMAs) to indicate changes in price momentum through the construction of an oscillator. The MACD can appear as two lines, the direction and crossovers of which give trading signals. It can also appear as a series of vertical bars known as a histogram. I use both MACD formats interchangeably when analyzing price momentum changes.

MACD was originally created by master Technical Analyst Gerald Appel. It is calculated by taking into account the difference between a longer-termed EMA and a shorter EMA. For instance, MACD can be constructed by subtracting the value of a 12-day EMA from a 26-day EMA. Then plot their difference daily as a solid line. This is known as the MACD line. Next calculate a nine-day EMA of the MACD line itself. Plot it daily as a different color or as a dashed line. The nine-day EMA of the MACD line is known as the signal line. The signal line, an EMA of the MACD line itself, is slower moving than the MACD line. Thus the MACD line is often called the fast line, and the signal line is often called the slow line.

Watch the MACD for divergence in direction between the MACD and the underlying security. As with other momentum indicators, if the MACD slopes downward while the security is forming higher highs (i.e., diverging), this can be a leading indicator toward a shift into the phase three topping period. Similarly, divergence by a rising MACD during a falling trend in the underlying security might be signaling a coming directional change to a phase one basing pattern for the security.

Crossovers of the fast and slow lines help identify pending directional changes for the underlying security. If the fast line rises and goes through the slow line, it means momentum is picking up. In that case, it's better to be long than short the security. If the fast line drops below the slow line, this means momentum is slowing. You may need to look for an exit.

Most charting software or Internet charting programs offer an option

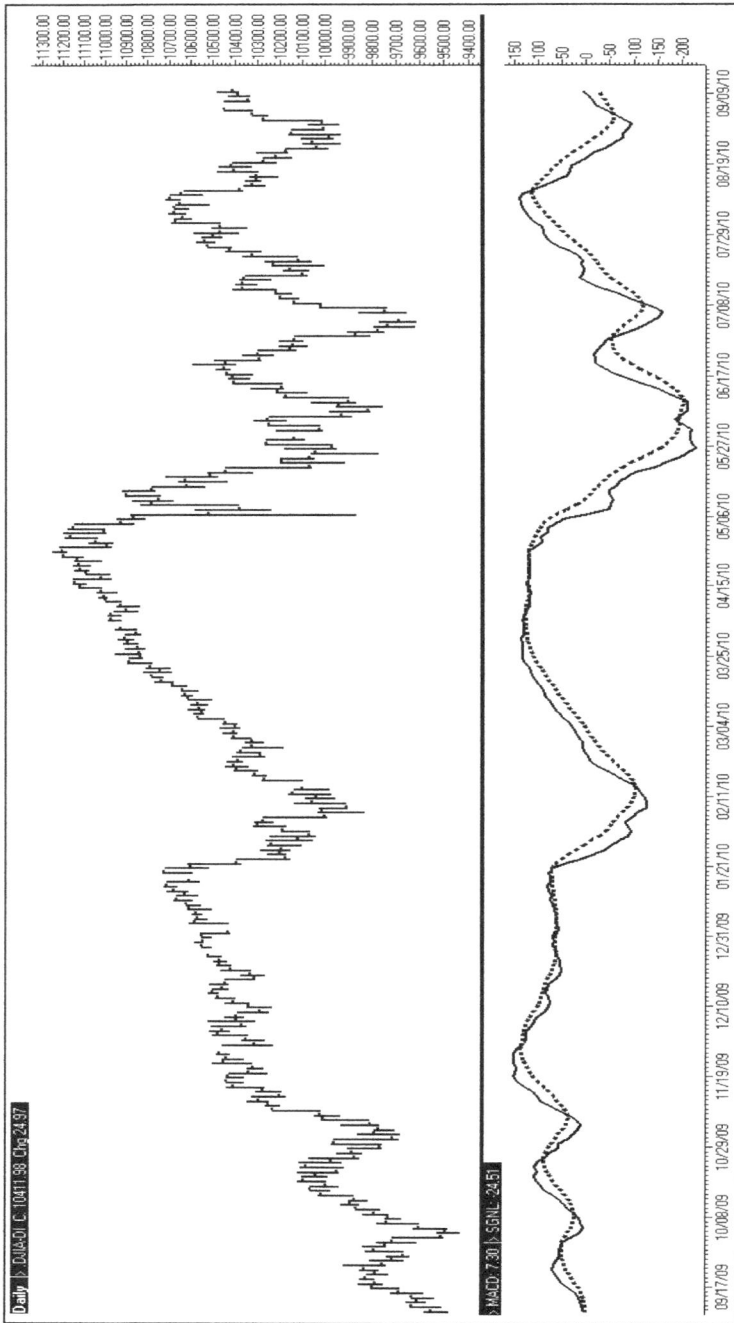

Figure 34. Daily chart of DJIA October 2009 to October 2010. Note how the solid MACD signal line provides very accurate buy signals when it crosses up through the dashed slower line. The bearish crossovers are a little less definable on this chart. (Copyright © 1988-2008, Thomson Financial)

to view MACD as a histogram. This can be easier to interpret and view compared with the original MACD format. As you know, the original plots the difference between the MACD (fast) line and the signal (slow) line. They appear as vertical bars in a separate window on your chart. You can also use the histogram format to identify divergences in slope between the MACD and the underlying security. It is an easy-to-interpret format. Crossovers and position above or below the zero line on a MACD histogram are less important than the *direction of the indicator's trend*. As always, look for the trend of the MACD line or histogram to confirm the direction of the market. If they diverge, this can signal a pending change in trend for the underlying security. Figure 34 above illustrates both types of MACD indicators.

I emphasize here that MACD, like all momentum indicators, is a tool to be used as additional input after identifying the security's phase, trend, and formation. MACD should not be used as a standalone.

In a Nutshell

Momentum indicators help you finesse your entry or exit points after you determine your initial phase, pattern, and cycle (discussed in the next chapter) identification. An overbought momentum indicator coinciding with a topping formation may indicate it's time to vacate the market. Similarly, a divergence in trend between a momentum indicator and the underlying security gives clues to a change in direction.

The Rate of Change indicator may be the most easily understood of them all. But many of the newer momentum indicators are superior tools for entry and exit timing. In this book I have chosen to focus on my two favorites, the RSI and MACD indicators. I find they work best for me. The RSI amply identifies overbought and oversold levels. Although I prefer to work with just a couple of momentum tools, this does not imply that you should choose to ignore the many alternative indicators that can help you identify overbought and oversold conditions. I encourage you to read Martin Pring's *Martin Pring on Momentum* to learn about other momentum indicators.

The next chapter deals with market cycles. There you will learn how big-picture tools can give you the background information you need to customize your trading strategies within the context of the lessons already learned in this book.

5

CYCLES

CYCLES exist throughout nature. Seasons rotate through winter, spring, summer, and fall. The cycle of life endlessly rotates from birth to death. The planets, and even the universe itself, eternally rotate through cycles.

Cycles also exist in the financial markets. No cycle repeats itself exactly. Rather than be concerned with slight variations in amplitude (the maximum deviation of measured data) and duration (the time over which the cycle occurs) of a cycle, you're better off to simply understand that cycles are the tendency of a pattern to repeat itself. We can count on cycles happening with a reasonable degree of predictability, repeating themselves over and over for an indefinite period.

Identifying a cycle occurring on the stock market is akin to identifying a seasonal weather pattern. For example, on the whole, we can say winter is cold and summer is hot. But sometimes we have very mild winters. Does a mild winter, or a late start to winter, equate to a discontinuation of the seasonal patterns? Or is it just an anomaly? Of course you know the answer to that question. A mild winter is a deviation from the norm – a miss of the current cycle, one could say. No need for anyone to push the panic button just yet.

Interestingly, should a stock market pattern fail to match its expected pattern in a given year, many investors will declare the end of that cycle. They'll say, "It just doesn't work anymore." Cycles of any sort work on the principle of averages. That is, on average, the cycle has proven to be reliable. Don't discount a market cycle just because it misses a beat, any more than you would throw away your snow shovels just because you experience a mild winter.

There are many cycles occurring in the broad markets as well as in individual sectors. It's important to note that knowledge of an existing cycle must not be used in isolation from other analytical methods. Use cyclical analysis in conjunction with the other tools presented in this book. For instance, consider the cyclical tendency to weak stock markets during the second year in the U.S. presidency. It might line up with a phase three topping pattern breakdown. On top of that, you might note the occurrence of a bearish momentum oscillator divergence and an oversold sentiment indicator reading (described later in this book). The odds of a move into a phase four downtrend increase when all of these factors are present.

As I've been emphasizing throughout this book, it's the confirmation and concurrence of various pieces of evidence that should dictate your trading decisions, not the presence of a single signal from an individual indicator or pattern.

Some Commonly Known Cycles

I'm going to focus on the basics and leave out a lot of the theory behind cycles, this being a practical book for investors. For a more detailed explanation on cycle theory, I recommend *The Profit Magic of Stock Transaction Timing* by J.M. Hurst.

Possibly the most commonly accepted cycle of interest to investors in the free markets is the economic business cycle. Economies tend to rotate between expansion, equilibrium, and contraction. It's similar to the way securities rotate between the four market phases. There are also much longer cycles than the business cycle that affect the markets. For example, consider the 50- to 54-year Kondratieff cycle originally discovered by Russian economist Nicolai Kondratieff. It contains an *up wave* of about 20 years, a *transition period* lasting seven to ten years, and a *down wave* of about 20 years. Again, this is similar to phase two, three, and four for the stock market.

In my first book, *SmartBounce*, I described another cycle known as the decennial pattern. It is the unexplainable tendency of years ending in certain digits to perform predictably. For example, there has never been a negative year ending in 5 since 1880; years ending in 7 and 0 are, on average, more often negative in performance.

Some investors follow the presidential election cycle. The theory behind this, originally developed by Yale Hirsch, suggests that U.S. stock markets are more likely to be weak during the first year following the election of a new president. Thereafter, the market should improve and the cycle begins again with a new election. This theory seems not to have held much water during recent presidencies – witness the strong stock market performance in the first year of George H. W. Bush's era, both starting years during Bill Clinton's era, and Obama's first year in office in 2009.

Another cycle, less known to most investors, may be of interest to those of us who trade Canadian equities. Here in Canada, my friend Grant Shorten, a Technical Analyst, wrote a research paper on a 185-day cycle that appears to accurately predict market troughs on the S&P TSX 300 stock index. See the Shorten Cycle in figure 35, below.

You will notice that it has had a few incorrect calls, the worst of which was the June 2008 market peak at a time when the Shorten Cycle indicated a trough. While the Shorten Cycle hasn't accurately predicted every major trough on the TSX since Grant wrote his original research paper back in 2003, it has proven to be worth tracking, when charting the index, in conjunction with the other tools described in this book. One of the more impressive troughs the cycle predicted was the precise trough low of the 2008-2009 bear market on March 3, 2009. The cycle caught the precise day of the bear market bottom.

Grant emailed me in late 2010 while I was doing the final editing of this book. His statistics suggest that by buying the day after the Shorten Cycle predicts the trough low and selling only if the TSX breaks below its 75-day SMA after 20 days of a buy signal, you can generate superior returns to a buy-and-hold strategy. The Shorten Cycle trading system (using the 75-day MA sell trigger) is not just about identifying potential buying opportunities at the troughs. It's about being out of the market during key downturns.

According to the Shorten Cycle, upcoming potential troughs should

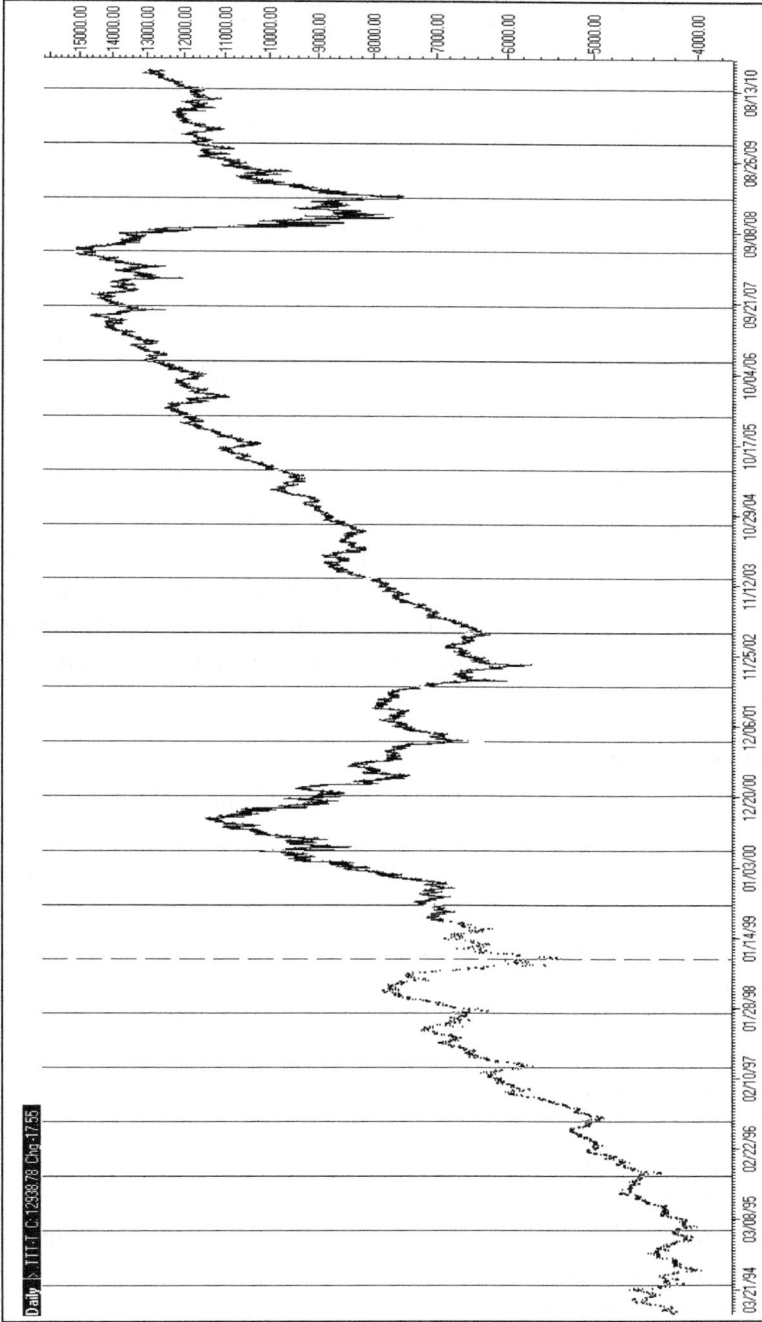

Figure 35. Chart of TSX with Shorten Cycle 1994 to 2010 with predicted troughs marked by vertical lines. (source?)

CYCLES

71

occur on May 27, 2011, February 22, 2012, and November 21, 2012.
I would like to emphasize again that you should combine any cycle
analysis with the other tools you've learned about in this book.

There's a four-year cycle that has been tracked back to 1854 by Larry
Williams, Technical Analyst and market timer. According to this cycle,
markets tend to experience an underperforming year every fourth year.
The cycle's underperforming year hit the markets in 2010. That lined up
with the decennial pattern tendency for years ending in 0 to be weaker.

The impact of any cycle, including the four-year cycle, is multiplied
when it coincides with another cycle. For example, if the fourth year of
the four-year cycle lands during the first year of a presidential term in
a year ending in 7, there may be a greater potential for the markets to
experience a negative performance.

The more factors reinforcing a market cycle, the more likely that
market cycle will live up to its potential. Imagine that the Dow trades
near the top of the larger sideways trading range established earlier in this
book. Then suppose other broad market timing tools approach expensive
levels. You could anticipate even greater potential for an underperforming
period to follow. Cycles are factors that definitely should be considered
when making investment decisions.

Composition of a Cycle

Cycles consist of bottoms, which are called troughs, and tops, which
are called peaks. I've used these terms repeatedly since we covered trend
analysis in chapter 1. We should measure the time period of a cycle from
trough to trough. Cycle peaks can end up slightly to the left or right of
the middle of a cycle. This can make peak measurement less accurate.
The potential for a peak to occur earlier or later in a cycle is known as
translation. The most important aspect of cycle analysis is to understand
that the validity of a cycle is tested by how close it comes to having
troughs equal time periods apart.

A cycle's *amplitude* is the average height of the waves within the
cycle. The greater the distance between the peaks and troughs of a cycle,
the greater the amplitude that cycle displays. Many different cycles occur
on the markets all the time. Some of these may bottom at the same time.
This is known as synchronicity. Suppose you see two cycles that seem to
have the same time period. You also note that they form troughs at

different moments in time. That difference is known as the phase difference between the two cycles or waves. As a practical trader using cycle analysis, ideally you want to identify cycles with sufficient amplitude to make trading the cycle worthwhile. In addition, you want to identify cycles with troughs that look as if they could occur at about the same time as the other phase, trend, and formation indicators you are using. That could supply more confirmation of a potential buying opportunity.

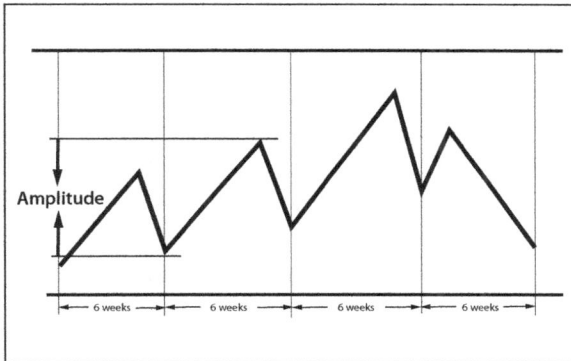

Figure 36. A basic cycle.

For my money, the most reliable and important cycles are seasonal cycles: the tendency of overall markets to outperform during certain times of the year, or for various sectors, such as gold or technology, to perform best at certain times of the year. For example, the broad stock market tends to be stronger between November and May. Then it often weakens at the beginning of summer. After that it briefly shows a bit of strength into midsummer, more often than not declining between August and November.

If you want to digger deeper, there are several books you should consider reading. Yale Hirsch and his son Jeffery Hirsch have done immense research on seasonal investing. Their book *Stock Trader's Almanac* is published yearly and should be in every investor's library. Canadian author Brooke Thackray has taken the Hirschs' work to a new level in his yearly publication *Thackray's Investment Guides*. Don Vialoux, the highly respected Technical Analyst, has also done independent work involving the identification of seasonal patterns on the markets.

I draw in this chapter on the work of these pioneers in the field of seasonal investing to present what I feel are the most important seasonal cycles for an intermediate- to long-term investor. There are many seasonal patterns that take place over various time spans right down to cycles occurring for only hours at a time on an intraday basis. We'll concentrate on those that last for at least three months. This way we can avoid excessive trading, focus on the larger moves of the markets, and ignore the shorter-term less-profitable cycles.

Best Six Months

I covered the Best Six Months strategy in my first book, *SmartBounce*, but would like to discuss it again here. *Stock Trader's Almanac* by Yale Hirsch identifies patterns showing that September and October are statistically poor-performing months. The author tracks results of investments made at the end of October, sold at the end of April, and with proceeds invested in Treasury bills for the remaining months. Results on major North American markets tracked from 1953 to the present prove the validity of seasonal market timing. This cycle works most years and on occasion underperforms. So it is important to stick with the program to reap the benefits over the long term. Brooke Thackray also tracks this cycle in his annual investment guides attempting to pinpoint more exact entry and exit points.

Thackray shows us that $10,000 invested in the Dow on October 28 and then switched into cash on May 5 every year from 1950 to 2008 would grow to $806,204 by the end of 2008. Astoundingly, the same $10,000 invested in the Dow during the worst six months (May 6 to October 27) would produce a loss of $535 during the same period. All of the positive returns (on a net basis) on the markets seem to occur between November and April.

Trading the Energy Cycle

Perhaps the most dominant of the seasonal sector rotations occurs in the energy sector. Oil prices, in particular, tend to bottom near the end of February. They tend to reach a peak in early May. Thackray explains that the cycle is based on the premise that the demand for oil increases as the driving season in the spring approaches. The oil sector has outperformed the S&P 500 during its seasonally strong period 92% of the time since

1984. It beats the S&P 500 by an average of 6%. To play the seasonal cycle on oil, buy oil, energy stocks, or energy-based exchange traded funds (ETFs) in February and sell them in May.

You may be unfamiliar with the term *correlation* as it applies to investment performance relationships. Think of it like this: a perfect correlation of 1.0 between two securities means that these securities move in lockstep with each other on a price performance basis. If the correlation is -1.0, that means the two securities move exactly opposite to each other in performance: a perfect negative correlation. If the correlation is 0, that implies there is no relationship at all between the two securities and that price movements of one security offer no clue to the price movements of the other. A correlation of 0 can also be called a non-correlated relationship. An excellent correlation analysis tool is available at www.investorcraft.com.

Gold and the Indian Wedding Season

According to seasonality expert Brooke Thackray, gold has outperformed the S&P 500 between July 27 and September 25 since 1984. He attributes this outperformance to the Indian festival and wedding season that starts in October and ends in November. Gold is considered the gift of choice for these festivals. Jewelry fabricators tend to stock up in the months before the festival season to allow time to create products for sale.

Playing the seasonal gold cycle can be an excellent hedge as the markets head into the often-weak months of August and September. But pay very close attention to the recent correlation of gold's performance in relationship to the stock market. For example, in 2008 and 2009, gold's traditional non-correlated performance with stocks changed to become somewhat correlated in performance with the stock market.

The Information-Technology Cycle

One of the things that appeals to me about seasonal investing is its basis in common sense. Seasonal cycles occur because crowds have predictable behavior as they become excited about various investment themes. Human beings seem to be myopic by nature. We can't see beyond our own noses when it comes to preparing for the inevitable changes the markets will deliver. The info-tech seasonal cycle is a perfect example of human emotion at work on the stock markets.

Info-tech stocks tend to outperform between early October and late January. Look to trade individual stocks or ETFs during this time frame to play this cycle. The sector does well during the October to January period due to the heightened awareness of new electronic devices promoted to consumers during the retail holiday shopping season. The huge electronics conferences and trade shows taking place during this time of the year add to the awareness of the sector. Your job as a trader is to exit your positions in the technology sector when the awareness and hype surrounding the new electronic devices is at its highest – typically at the end of January.

Trading the Consumer Staples/Discretionary Cycle

Another dominant seasonal trend is the positive performance of consumer discretionary stocks compared with broader markets from late October to late April. After that, consumer staples outperform from May to November. Obviously, this creates a swap opportunity. Here one could buy and sell the respective ETFs for these sectors by rotating back and forth between them every year. Thackray surmises that the rotation of strength between these two sectors occurs due to a positive wealth effect from rising portfolio values during the previously discussed Best Six Months cycle. When consumers feel wealthy, they are more inclined to make discretionary spending choices. In summer when markets are weaker, consumers will stick with staples and not spend too frivolously. This swap is one of my favorites, one I do religiously every year.

Elliott Wave Theory

Some Technical Analysts specialize in predicting future market activity by using Elliott Wave Theory (EWT). The theory, created by Ralph Nelson Elliott, was made popular largely by Robert Prechter Jr., a modern Technical Analyst. EWT has been around since 1939. It became much more popular after Prechter successfully predicted the emergence of the last bull market in 1982.

The theory is fairly complex, in many respects, but its basic premises can be understood by most investors. Before covering it, I'd like to point out that Elliott Wave analysis is a very subjective tool open to many differing interpretations. If you put four different Elliott Wave analysts in a room and tell them to predict market movements through their wave-counts and calculated retracements, you'll get four different answers. Learn to understand the basic concepts of crowd psychology present behind each of the waves that Elliott describes in his theory, but don't attempt to estimate the current Elliott wave position for use in timing your entry and exit strategies.

EWT can be an excellent tool to get a feel for what phase the market is in. It does not, in my opinion, offer a clear indication of how and when we might trade within that phase. Use the tools presented earlier in this book to support your trading decisions. Use Elliott Wave analysis to provide more background to help you understand current market behavior.

EWT postulates that markets move within a five-wave pattern in the major trend. These waves, called impulse waves, are typically labeled by EWT analysts from one to five. The five-wave pattern in a dominant cycle is seen during strongly trending phase two bull markets and phase four bear markets.

After the five-wave impulse waves, we can observe three waves going against the major trend. These are called corrective waves. EWT analysts label these movements with the letters a, b, and c. Each wave, whether it is an impulse wave or a corrective wave, can be broken down to similar five- and three-wave patterns within themselves. This can get very confusing for the average investor. Furthermore, sideways patterns emerge when the three corrective waves repeat themselves over and over again as a, b, c, x, a, b, c, x, etc. The three corrective a, b, and c waves, along with their more complex sideways patterns, form the patterns discussed earlier in this book. I've included some diagrams in the following pages to help demonstrate these five- and three-wave concepts.

Wave counts can be confusing. Throw in their Fibonacci mathematical relationships and things get even more complex. I'm not going to talk about Fibonacci here – besides, I am not convinced that this tool is useful. My main use for EWT is to understand how the distinct characteristics of each of these waves can give a rough idea of where the market might be within its dominant cycle.

For example, the major trend from 1982 to 1999 was a phase two bull market. In 2000, the market changed to a sideways market. During the 1982-1999 bull market, the major trend was up. An Elliott Wave Analyst would argue that it went up in the five-wave pattern. Accordingly, you can get a feel for which of the five waves the market was in at the time by observing the mood of the market.

Wave One

The first wave of the EWT five-wave sequence usually represents the most tepid of the five-wave pattern. It is the start of a new market trend: a new bull market or the entry into phase two as described earlier in this book. At the beginning of a new bull market, the media are still largely printing negative news. Daily price volatility is high, but volume on the up days is not rising enough to convince investors the market has entered a new uptrend. In the last bull market, it looks as if wave one begins in 1982 and ends in 1987.

Wave Two

The second wave corrects gains of the first one. As in standard trend analysis (see chapter 1), the pullback or corrective wave must not extend below the starting point of wave one. In other words, we need to see a higher low, now that we've had a higher high in wave one! This pullback brings shouts of glee from the bears who say, "See – we told you the recent rally was a false start. Things are still bad out there!" In the meantime, a few positive bits of news make their way into the media. Some Elliotticians feel 1987 was a wave two corrective wave. All corrective waves, including wave two of the five-wave sequence, break down into three smaller a, b, and c sub waves, as illustrated in figure 37 below.

Wave Three

This is the big one. Here positive news about the economy finally shows up in the news in a big way. Analysts finally start to raise earnings projections. Stocks are rising and pullbacks are short-lived with low volume. Wave three brings the crowd back into the market, making it the longest-lived and strongest of the five-wave bull market. In the last bull market, wave three may have begun after the 1987 correction ending in 1998. Due to the subjective nature of EWT, there is a variety of opinions about whether the wave three bull market phase ended in 1998 or at a multitude of other corrective points. The point here is that the biggest move and easiest money were made mostly during the last bull market in the 1990s.

Wave Four

This is another corrective wave. It can be fairly weak and present itself as a meandering market rather than a full pullback. Its movement from peak to trough is fairly small. Some might argue that the 1998 "Asian Contagion" stock market pullback was a wave four corrective movement. As with all corrective waves, wave four should break down into three smaller a, b, and c sub waves.

Wave Five

All wave fives are characterized by a raging bullishness that eventually comes to the final blow-out ending of the bull market. Every fool with a dollar in his or her hand has to buy a stock. Moreover, it's always a stock bubble that characterizes the fifth wave. Breadth, which is the measurement of total participation by all stocks on the market, is poor. Fewer stocks do all of the work. Meanwhile, the majority of stocks underperform.

In the last bull market ending in 1999, it was technology stocks that created wave five. If you didn't own tech stocks at that time, you were not in the game. Just as the crowd shouts their cries of disbelief when a new bull market emerges in wave two, the wave five crowd quickly ridicules any bears forecasting the end of the bull market. Contrarians are not very popular during EWT wave fives.

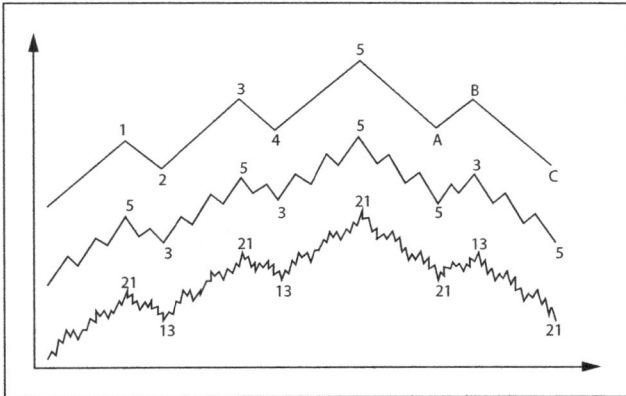

Figure 37. Diagram of five impulse waves up and three corrective waves down broken into sub-waves.

In a Nutshell

In this chapter you learned the basics of cycles. I focused on a few of the most reliable cycles I have used successfully in my practice as a discretionary Portfolio Manager for ValueTrend Wealth Management. Cycles you should be aware of include the Presidential Cycle, the Economic Cycle, the Four-year Cycle, and the Decennial pattern.

We also introduced you to Elliott Wave Theory. EWT is a useful tool to get a feel for the current phase of the market. It works best to identify the mood of the crowd, as a tool to measure mass psychology. As such, I believe it is of less use for identifying the phase of an individual security.

The theory is that markets move in five impulse waves that occur within a phase two bull markets. That's followed by three corrective wave patterns. They may represent a phase three topping pattern, a phase four bear market, or a phase one basing pattern. These waves have measurable relationships to each other, known as Fibonacci mathematical relationships. Each wave is characterized by certain crowd behavior.

It's here that EWT is most useful to pragmatic traders. Watching the mood of the crowd can give vital clues where we may be in the EWT pattern. For example, if the crowd aggressively speculates on one or two sectors after a long bull market, the market may be in the wave five bubble stage.

The most practical cycles for traders exist in seasonal investing patterns. In this chapter, we discussed the Best Six Months Cycle followed by four distinctly reliable seasonal sector trades. Each of these sector trades is based on logical buying and selling patterns arising from underlying fundamental conditions.

Learning to identify new cycles is a subject for an entire book. If you want to learn more about cycles, check out *The Profit Magic of Stock Transaction Timing* by J.M Hurst.

The next chapter covers some other very useful market timing tools. They will help you identify ideal entry and exit points within the context of the investment climate and individual security analysis.

SIDEWAYS

6

OTHER TOOLS

IN the movie *Wall Street*, starring Michael Douglas and Martin Sheen, Douglas's character, Gordon Gekko, states that "greed is good."

He may have a point. In its basic form, greed helps drive individuals to add value to other people's lives by offering goods and services that they want. These goods and services are provided by entrepreneurs and large businesses in pursuit of creating wealth for themselves and their shareholders.

For an investor or trader, however, greed – and its counterpoint, fear – are not good. In fact, these emotions are counterproductive in the pursuit of market profits. We learn to separate ourselves from these emotions by sticking to our trading plan and utilizing the proven analytical tools described in this book.

Interestingly, there is a way that we can profit from the emotions of fear and greed that *other* market participants are experiencing. We can utilize a unique set of technical tools known as contrarian indicators.

Contrarian Indicators

Contrarian indicators, also known as sentiment indicators, attempt to identify the point of maximum optimism, or "irrational exuberance," as a former Federal Reserve Chairman once called it. High levels of optimism by market participants usually coincide with market tops. A contrarian indicator can also identify the point of maximum pessimism, which is usually demonstrated by total capitulation by the investing public. Maximum pessimism typically occurs at market bottoms or troughs.

Contrarian indicators, when combined with other tools you have learned to use, can help identify ideal entry and exit points on the broad markets. They can provide an almost unfathomable level of accuracy.

Because the crowd usually gets it wrong, we know to exit the market when our contrarian tools signal "too many happy faces," as one of my clients once put it, and to enter when these tools signal high levels of anxiety, fear, and capitulation by investors and traders.

I would like to point out that we should never begrudge the herd mentality of retail investors, investment advisors, and mutual fund managers. After all, somebody has to buy our stocks as markets get too high! If these fine folks weren't bullish at the wrong time, who would buy our stocks when we feel it's time to get out? Conversely, if the crowd wasn't despondently selling their securities at bargain-basement prices, where would our cheap entry points come from?

Personally, I love these people for the wealth they have helped me create for me and my clients. It's a symbiotic relationship when you really think about it.

Some more widely used contrarian indicators include surveys of newsletter writers' opinions, the ratio of short positions to long positions on a stock exchange, and put to call option trading comparisons. Let's take a look at two of the more readily available contrarian indicators you can begin using today.

Smart Money vs. Dumb Money

In the 1990s, Merrill Lynch Canada's Technical Analyst Gurney Watson was tracking a technical analysis tool called the Smart Money/Dumb Money Indicator (SMDM). He created his version of the indicator to track the movement of various U.S. indices during two distinct time frames: the first hours of trading (morning) and the last hours of trading (afternoon). Mr. Watson would chart the net gain or loss during the first two hours of the trading day and compare it with the net gain or loss during the last two trading hours of the day. He labeled trading done in the early part of the day as dumb money activity and trading being done in the latter part of the day as smart money activity.

The theory is that, during the first part of the trading day, retail investors tend to execute trades based less on an analytical process and more on an emotional, unsophisticated basis. Retail investors often base trades on recent news events and react quickly with fear or greed to their trading executions. These emotionally-driven market movers are anxious to call their broker to execute their trades within the first few hours of the day in response to the hot news of the moment.

Conversely, sophisticated traders, including market professionals, are more apt to trade using mechanical analysis programs to eliminate their emotions when making investment decisions. These investors are less inclined to react to their own fear and greed. According the SMDM theory, sophisticated traders take advantage of the rabid selling or buying done during the early hours of the trading day. By the end of the day, the net effect of the large buying or selling power resulting from the professionals' activity drives the market up or down in a direction opposite to the one created in the morning.

According to SMDM theory, the trick in determining which way the market might be heading in the near future is to watch the net movements of the indices during these periods of the day. Often there is little consistency in patterns of SMDM movement when the market is either trending (up or down) or trading sideways. However, at market peaks and troughs, emotional trading in the morning escalates. Sophisticated investors begin to take advantage of this trading.

Obviously, as investors, it's better for us to follow the smart money and do the opposite of the dumb money.

Suppose we notice, over a period of several trading days, that there is a fairly obvious pattern in which smart afternoon money is bidding the market higher than it was in the morning. This may be a sign that going long on the market is prudent.

Conversely, if we see the afternoon markets are lower than the morning, we may want to consider bearish strategies, such as holding cash, hedging existing positions, or (for aggressive investors) shorting the market.

You can track smart money versus dumb money manually, or or by subscribing to www.sentimenttrader.com. They use the first half hour of the day's trading as dumb money and the last hour as smart money. This website offers its subscribers a huge variety of sentiment indicators with expert commentary and interpretation.

ISEE Options Indicator

Back in the late 1990s, I researched the profitability of combining the classic "put to call" ratio with the RSI sentiment indicator (discussed in the momentum chapter of this book). My research, which I submitted to the Market Technicians Association in New York, ultimately helped me earn my credentials as a Chartered Market Technician. History proves we can experience a very high level of market timing success by combining these two indicators.

The ISEE indicator offered by International Securities Exchange is a very useful contrarian tool. You can access the ISEE indicator free at www.ise.com. The indicator shows the ratio of call buyers versus put buyers on the ISE options exchange. It is refined to exclude pro traders and market makers. Puts are bought by investors who seek to profit if the market on an underlying security falls. Calls are bought by investors who think the underlying security will rise.

A rising ISEE indicator number indicates relatively increasing interest in call options compared with put options. Conversely, a falling ISEE number indicates relatively decreasing interest in calls compared with puts.

My research shows when the ISEE indicator gets around 150 for a few days in a row, the markets may be getting too bullish and are due for a correction. If the ISEE indicator drops below 80 for a few days, it suggests an oversold market that may be ready to rally. Look for clusters where the ISEE indicator reaches these extreme levels for three of the past four trading days. They don't have to occur concurrently.

Combining ISEE Sentiment Readings
with RSI Momentum

You can combine the ISEE indicator with another to refine your entry and exit points for the stock market. For example, suppose you spot an RSI momentum reading over 70 on a daily chart of the S&P 500 (or the DJIA) while also noting an ISEE reading of 150 for a few days. You can strongly infer a correction of some magnitude is due on the markets. Consider reducing equities at that time. Conversely, an RSI reading of 30 and an ISEE reading of 80 for a few days usually indicates a strong buying opportunity. As a rule of thumb:

> BUY if RSI = 30 & ISEE = 80
> SELL if RSI = 70 & ISEE = 150

Chicago Board Options Exchange Volatility Index (VIX)

I would be remiss if I did not mention, in the context of of market sentiment timing tools, the popular VIX indicator. The VIX predicts implied volatility of S&P 500 index options for the next 30 days. In essence, a high VIX indicator reading corresponds with higher market volatility and more costly options. A low VIX reading corresponds with lower market volatility and cheaper options.

The VIX is sometimes incorrectly referred to as "the fear index." (A few of my trading friends sometimes call the VIX "the vomit index" – high VIX levels can cause vertigo in market participants.) Instead of being an indication of capitulation or overt bullishness, the VIX simply predicts volatility in either direction. High VIX levels suggest that options traders see significant potential for the market to move sharply, either up or down.

You want to watch the VIX, therefore, if you feel, based on your analysis, that the market has become overextended in either direction. A market that appears to be overextended and making a top might be verified by a high VIX reading. Conversely, a market that has sold off aggressively and might be ready to bottom could could be verified by a high VIX reading.

Personally, I have not found a universally acceptable high level on the VIX to indicate a high enough point to reliably correspond with a market top or bottom. Some traders use moving averages to smooth the VIX. They have devised various ways to interpret levels for trading signals.

OTHER TOOLS

I advise you to note levels that the VIX attains at key market turning points in recent history. This will give you some indication of the levels to look for as a backup turning-point indicator. At the risk of sounding like a broken record, let me remind you that the VIX, as with all indicators, is just one more tool in your analysis process. It should not be considered a stand-alone decision-making device for trading.

Breadth Indicators

It's easy to find out if the market is moving up in a broad manner or not. There are market breadth indicators like the Advance/Decline line, the 52-Week High/Low line, the cumulative volume index, and volume-based breadth indicators. They all use the total number of advancing stocks and declining stocks to determine the level of participation in the market's movement. They graphically indicate whether the market has a broad cross-section of participants.

Strong breadth within a rising market confirms a strong bull market.

Weak breadth, in the midst of a rising stock market, can alert us that the bull market may be coming to an end. Weak breadth means there are more stocks going down than up.

I noted in *SmartBounce* that this happened in 2007 when the NYSE Advance/Decline line peaked in July and began to decline thereafter. Meanwhile, the Dow and S&P 500 kept rising until they reached all-time high levels in October of that year. That meant money was flowing into a very concentrated number of stocks that had a greater influence on these indices. The Advance/Decline line gave us three months' notice of an impending problem with overall market breadth. That was plenty of time to reduce our exposure to the equity markets before the 2008/2009 crash.

Most breadth indicators are available in your charting software. They can be accessed for free on a variety of financial websites on the Internet, including www.stockcharts.com and www.freestockcharts.com. I'll cover my favorite breadth indicators next, and show you how to interpret them.

Advance/Decline Line

The Advance/Decline indicator is referred to as the A/D line by most Technical Analysts. This line cumulatively plots, on a daily basis, the total number of advancing issues minus the declining issues for a given market. These data are sometimes smoothed with a short moving average to make it a bit easier to see the prevailing trend of the line. Interpretation of this indicator is pretty straightforward.

If the A/D line slopes down while the market is climbing, the market is focused on too narrow a group of stocks. This almost invariably indicates that the market is setting up for a top and eventual reversal.

If the A/D line slopes up while the market is heading up, the A/D line is confirming a healthy, broadly-based uptrend that is likely to continue for the time being.

New High/Low Line

The 52-Week New High/Low line cumulatively plots, on a daily basis, all stocks on a market that have reached a high price point for the 52-week trading period minus the stocks that have made 52-week lows. The New High/Low line is a little slower to pick up a change in market breadth compared with the A/D line just discussed. For that reason, I find it less sensitive to predicting changes in today's fast-moving markets. Nonetheless, peek at it once in a while to use as another potential trend-reversal signal for the broad markets. Interpretation of this indicator is the same as for the A/D line. Any divergences in slope of the New High/Low line in relation to the market index price line should be interpreted as an indication of a pending change in trend direction.

Cumulative Volume Index

The Cumulative Volume Index, or CVI, is similar to the above indicators. Rather than determining breadth by *price*, it plots breadth by comparing *up volume* versus *down volume*. As with the A/D and New High/Low lines, CVI is calculated cumulatively. That means each day's value is added to the previous day's value. Up volume (the number of shares traded on losing stocks) is reduced by subtracting down volume (the number of shares traded on gaining stocks) on a daily basis. The result of that calculation is then added (or subtracted, if it is a negative number) to the prior day's plot on the chart.

As with all breadth indicators, look for a divergence in the direction of the line's slope compared with the slope of the market as warning of a trend reversal for the broad markets. Note that the CVI is not always easy to find for free on the Internet. Look at www.FreeStockCharts.com for a free plot of this indicator as well as many others.

OTHER TOOLS

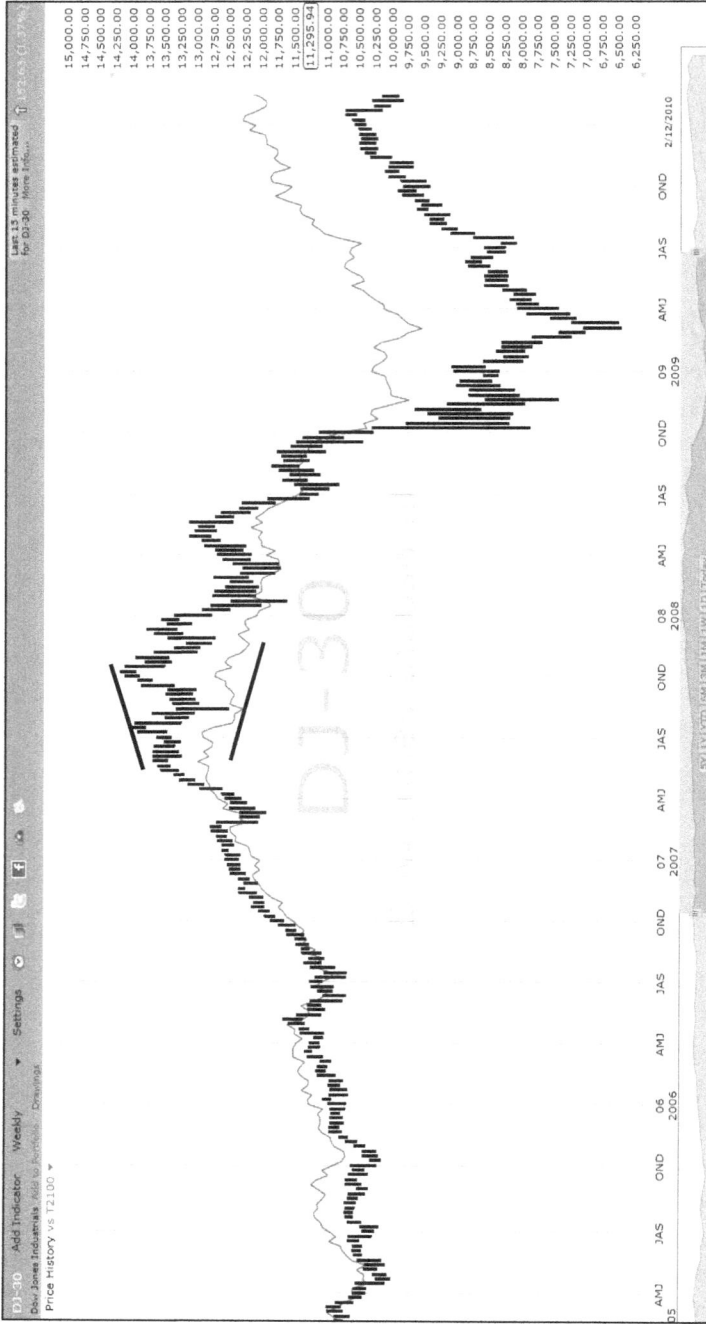

Figure 38. Chart of cumulative Advance/Decline line, vs. DJIA October 2005 to October 2008. I've marked the divergence between the Dow, which was making new highs between July and November of 2007, versus the A/D line, which made a lower low over the same period. This gave us some warning of the pending crash. (Courtesy of FreeStockCharts.com)

The Shiller Cyclically Adjusted PE Ratio

It may seem a bit out of place to use a classic fundamental analysis ratio as a market timing tool. But that's precisely what the Shiller PE ratio can help you do.

The commonly used Price to Earnings ratio (PE ratio) measures the price you pay for every dollar of earnings per share. The higher a PE ratio, the more expensive the market is. For example, a stock priced at $20 that earns $2 per share has a PE ratio of 10 ($20 / $2 = 10). A stock priced at $10 per share that earns $0.50/share has a PE ratio of 20 ($10 / $0.50 = 20). The lower-priced $10 stock is actually more expensive than the $20 stock because you are paying twice as much for every dollar in earnings.

While analysts usually hesitate to compare stocks in different industries with this valuation method, they will often use the PE ratio to compare how expensive or cheap a stock (or stock market index) is in relationship to its own PE history or to that of another company in the same industry.

Noted economist Robert Shiller of the Yale University economics department calculates a very interesting version of the time-honored PE ratio. His PE ratio, known as the Cyclically Adjusted PE, is calculated by using the ten-year average of earnings for U.S. equity markets, rather than using the past 12 months' earnings as is the common practice.

Shiller's data go back to 1881 to give us a true picture of stock market valuation history. The data are adjusted for inflation to keep the data accurate for interpretation today. As with the traditional PE ratio used by most analysts, the higher the PE ratio, the more overvalued the market. Conversely, a low PE ratio is considered a sign of an undervalued market.

Shiller's CAPE uses historical earnings data rather than forward-looking earnings data. I feel this gives an even more realistic picture of stock market valuation. I strongly believe that forward earnings data (earnings projections that analysts are estimating for the coming 12 months) are less accurate for calculating the PE ratio. The future is an unknown, whereas the past is a known factor.

The long-term average PE ratio for the stock market is around 16, using Shiller's calculations. Typically, when Shiller's CAPE ratio rises too much over 20, markets are becoming overvalued. Historically, there have only been two instances in which Shiller's CAPE ratio was able to rise past the mid 20s. In the year 1929, CAPE went above 30, and in 1999, PE went above 40. Both times markets were led into significant crashes. PE ratios of 20 to 25 more common and have accurately signaled numerous market corrections – including the recent 2008-2009 crash.

Stock market valuations become highly attractive when PE ratios move below ten. Shiller's CAPE troughed at levels below ten and signaled the onset of strong bull markets in 1921, 1932, 1974, and 1982. Use the Shiller CAPE ratio to provide input when when you're trying to determine the current valuation on the markets. As the ratio reaches 20 or higher, the more risky the overall market. Conversely the closer the ratio is to ten, the less risky. A PE around the mid-teens implies average valuation on the stock markets.

I find Shiller's work to be of enormous help when combined with the technical tools we've covered. If you recognize a potential phase three topping action after a rather frothy stock market (i.e., the end of a wave five in the Elliott sequence), you may be able to verify your observations through use of the Shiller CAPE ratio. If it reads too much over 20, this suggests an overvalued market. It may be ready for a trend change to the downside.

You can access the Shiller CAPE chart, along with many other very helpful fundamental indicator charts at no cost at www.multpl.com. I've included a recent CAPE chart from multpl.com below. You may notice the ratio has tended to contract (indicating a falling stock market) after reaching around 24 to 25 in every year except 1929 and 1999, as mentioned above.

In a Nutshell

This chapter introduced you to three new types of stock market timing tools: contrarian indicators, breadth indicators, and the Shiller CAPE ratio. Each of these tools is designed to provide input on the health of the overall stock market. Don't use them as stand-alone indicators to provide entry and exit signals but as strong back-ups for your already-thorough analysis of the trends, formations, and price momentums that you've observed on your index stock charts.

Contrarian indicators such as the ISEE index and the VIX are sentiment indicators. They offer a way to measure the current emotional state of the markets. The use of contrarian indicators for market timing is

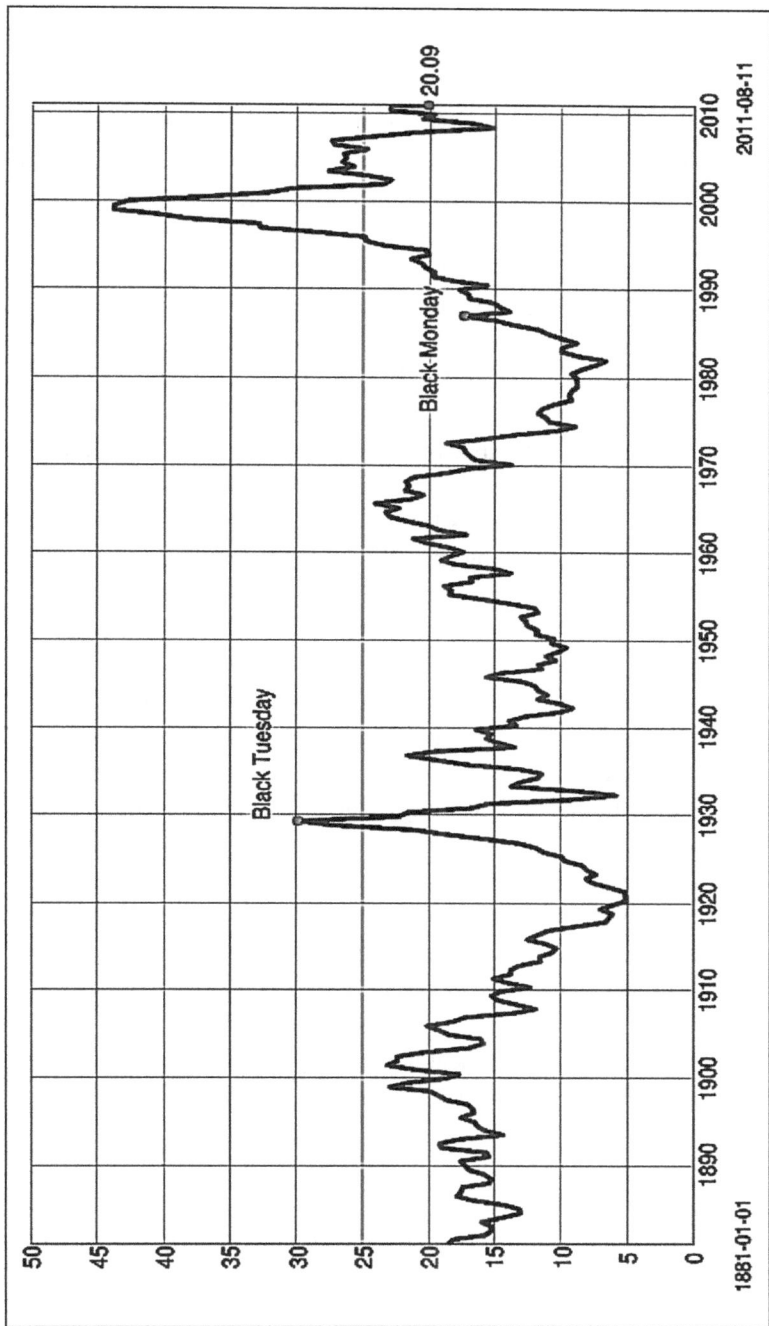

Figure 39. Shiller PE chart. (Courtesy of multpl.com)

OTHER TOOLS

based on the idea that the crowd is usually doing the wrong thing at the wrong time. They rabidly employ bullish strategies, such as buying call options, at market tops. They embrace bearish strategies, such as buying put options, at market bottoms. We can measure the level of trading by bulls versus bears through their call and put option trading. That gives us usable data that can indicate whether the market has become too bullish or bearish – a contrarian indicator.

Breadth indicators show whether the stock market is rising (or falling) through many different sectors and stocks. They can reveal if market participants are mainly interested in just a few select sectors. A market that is rising on only a few select stocks is probably in a bubble. A healthy stock market rises on a wide variety of issues. The A/D line, the New High/Low line, and the Cumulative Volume index are three of the more popular breadth indicators available to monitor market participation. Interpretation is simple: just look for breadth to rise with the market. If the market is rising on falling breadth, this means a very concentrated group of stocks is doing the work. A bubble may be forming. So you should be looking for other signs that indicate a phase three top may be forming.

The last broad market indicator you learned about was Robert Shiller's Adjusted PE ratio. This indicator avoids many of the flaws associated with the standard PE ratio used by most analysts over the years and is a highly accurate market-timing tool. Readings over 20 should cause you to sit up and take notice. A phase four market correction is on its way. Conversely, readings below ten almost invariably mean an undervalued market that is due for a phase two bull market. Readings between those two extremes are less definitive in interpretation. Nonetheless, be aware of the potential for market reversals as these extremes are approached – even if they're not penetrated.

The next chapter takes a look at Japanese Candlestick charting, which offers a quick and easy way to identify short-termed trends and reversals.

7

JAPANESE CANDLESTICK CHARTS

CANDLESTICK charts have an interesting history.
This highly visual form of charting technique has been in use by Japanese
traders since the 18th century. Candlestick charts are popular among
modern Technical Analysts for ease of use in reading and interpreting
chart patterns. I use candlestick charts in place of common bar charts
for almost all of my technical analysis.

My aim in this chapter is to provide you with enough knowledge
about this highly pragmatic form of charting to allow you to add a new
dimension to your technical analysis.

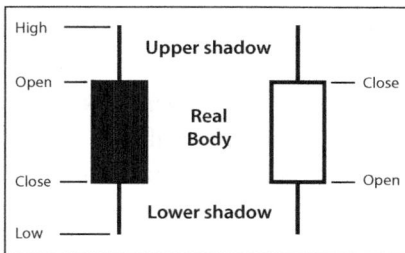

Figure 40. Candlestick chart.

Candlesticks are composed
of a real body and an upper and
lower wick, as illustrated here.

The so-called real body of a
candlestick is represented by the
area between the open and the
close prices of the period being
examined. Thus a daily chart has
candles with bodies composed

of the open and close of the day. A black body indicates that the security closed lower than its open. A white body indicates a close that was higher than the opening price. The upper wick of a candle represents the highest price the market traded for the day. The lower wick represents the lowest price for the day. If the market doesn't trade above or below its opening or closing prices, there is no wick on either end of the candle.

Here's the beauty of candlesticks: with one glance you can detect patterns that otherwise would be indiscernible on a standard bar chart. For example, a long candlestick body emphasizes a significant move (up or down, depending on the color). A series of long bodies moving in a trend suggests market strength plus a likely continuation of the trend for the time being. Conversely, short bodies represent indecision and a lack of price volatility. This lack of commitment by traders may indicate a pending change in trend. These small bodies are known as spinning tops.

There are many candlestick patterns that investors and traders can use to aid in selection of entry and exit decisions. In this chapter, I provide some of the basic patterns you can quickly learn to recognize and use when viewing candlestick charts. Get to know these patterns. They are very useful trading tools that few traders utilize properly. You gain an edge over other investors by incorporating candlestick pattern recognition into your toolkit. I recommend Steve Nison's classic book *Japanese Candlestick Charting Techniques* for a comprehensive and highly interesting read on candlestick charting.

Hammers and Hanging Men

Most significant candlestick formations are reversal patterns. One of the more useful reversal signals to come from candlestick analysis is the hammer formation. It can also be called the hanging man formation,

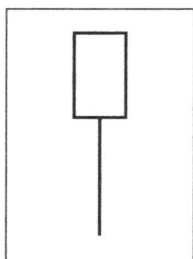

Figure 41. Hammer.

depending on where it occurs on the chart. These single candlestick patterns are characterized by a small real body located at or very close to the top of the candle. Western chartists experience a similar pattern. They refer to it as a key reversal day. This occurs when they see a bar on a chart that displays an open and close near the top of its trading range after a day with a violent amount of downside volatility.

Whatever you choose to call it, these single-bar formations represent a reversal signal that should not be ignored.

The high-bodied candlestick is usually a bullish formation if it occurs during a downtrend. When a trend reversal occurs to the upside, the formation is called a hammer.

The same candle formation is considered a bearish topping signal when it occurs during an uptrend. It's called a hanging man and signals the end of the uptrend.

The color of the real body is not vital to signify whether this candlestick is signaling a top or a bottom. But more often than not, you'll find black-bodied hanging man tops and white-bodied hammer bottoms. This is due to a change in sentiment during that trading day as it moves from bullish to bearish (hanging man) or bearish to bullish (hammer).

Shooting Stars and Inverted Hammers

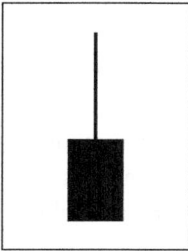

Figure 42.
Shooting stars and
inverted hammers.

Shooting stars and inverted hammers are upside-down versions of the hammer and hanging men patterns described above. Instead of the small real bodies being on the top in these patterns, they are on the bottom. Shooting star and inverted hammer candles exhibit long wicks on top of their real bodies. Shooting stars are topping formations and inverted hammers are bottoming formations. It doesn't matter what color the bodies are, but I've found that shooting stars are often black-bodied while inverted hammers are often white-bodied.

In both of these patterns, the real bodies should gap away from the real body of the previous day's trading.

Engulfing and Harami Patterns

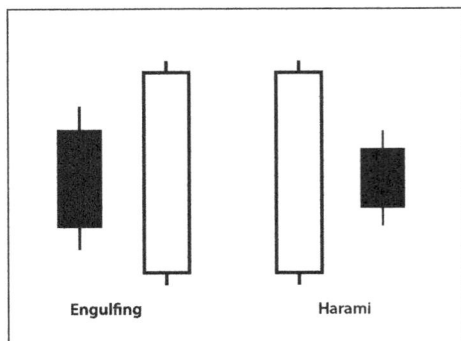

Figure 43. Engulfing and harami.

The engulfing pattern is another reversal pattern seen in candlestick formations. The two-step pattern consists of a smaller real body on the first candle, followed by a second with a larger real body the length of which brackets the first body from the top and bottom to engulf it. The second candle body is typically opposite in color to the first candle.

Uptrends about to change to a downtrend often have a black-bodied candle as the second (engulfing) candle in the formation. Downtrends about to change into an uptrend often have a white-bodied candle as the second candle. As the crowd's sentiment changes, the larger engulfing candle reflects the new direction to come. The larger the second candle body, the more likely the pattern will result in a trend reversal. Western chartists refer to a similar pattern on a standard bar chart as an "outside day."

Harami patterns reverse the order of engulfing patterns. Instead of a large body engulfing a preceding small body, a small body is engulfed by a preceding larger body. The larger the first body compared with the second, the more likely the reversal is to occur. The first candle body overlaps the top and bottom of the second. As a general observation, I find that engulfing patterns are more reliable reversal patterns than Harami patterns.

Morning and Evening Stars

Morning stars are bullish three-step patterns. They consist of a small-bodied candle gapping below the body of a preceding tall black candle.

That smaller candle is followed by a tall white candle that gaps above the preceding small one.

Evening stars are a bearish three-step pattern that consist of a small-bodied candle that gaps above the body of a preceding tall white candle body. That small candle is followed by a tall black candle that gaps below it. Both of these three-step patterns appear to leave the middle, smaller-bodied, candle in isolation due to the gaps on both sides.

The morning and evening doji stars are even more powerful reversal patterns. Doji stars are simply candles with little or no real body. The opening and closing price of the market are the same or very close to it. Any type of star that is isolated by a gap between the prior candle and the following candle is an extremely powerful reversal signal. It looks like an isolated star.

Western chartists call this occurrence an "island reversal," whereas candlestick chartists call it the "abandoned baby" pattern. Either name implies the same thing: the market has completely reversed its sentiment from the previous direction. Expect it to trend strongly in the opposite direction.

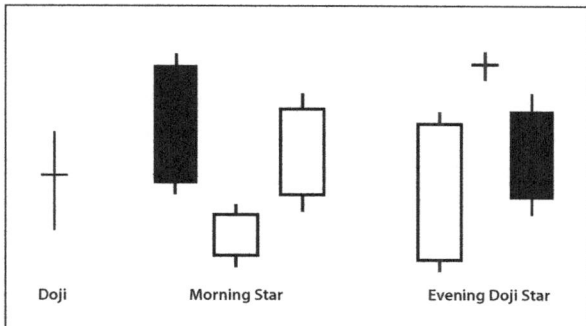

Figure 44. Doji, morning star, and evening doji star.

Computerized Fundamental Analysis

Computers offer the go-alone investor much of the power of large institutional investors on a fraction of the budget. Plan to spend about $1,000 or so per year for decent stock-screening software. This is peanuts compared with the typical management fees charged by investment products and mutual funds to manage a six-figure portfolio. Computer software searches through thousands of stocks for candidates meeting your needs. A good software program offers "black box" screens that look for a preselected set of criteria. As well, you can custom-screen with your own set of variables. Some programs focus exclusively on technical analysis. Others focus on fundamental factors such as "value stocks" or "earnings momentum stocks."

For example, you might be interested in finding stocks that are paying high dividends while displaying some earnings momentum. You can customize the computer program to screen thousands of stocks and select only those that meet these criteria. You may want to set criteria for eventually selling those stocks. Be aware that the sell criteria you create for the stocks could force their sale when earnings momentum drops below a certain level.

Note that you want to use the software to back-test the effectiveness of the criteria you've selected before committing to a system. In back testing, you check the historic profitability of your screening system. In effect, you simulate using the program to trade over a number of years.

You also want to note the *maximum* drawdown the system generates over those simulated years. Drawdown is defined as the reduction in value of your trading account between a high and low point over a given period. For example, in back-testing for the past decade, you might notice that the trading criteria in your system generated a five-month period in which the portfolio lost 30% of its value – the maximum drawdown for the decade. You might also observe that the program generates three other drawdowns of between 10% to 15% that last a month or so each time. You can now determine if that level of volatility is acceptable in the context of the longer-term rates of return that your system has delivered.

For stock screening with fundamental analysis tools, take a look at Vectorvest (www.vectorvest.com), Valueline (www.valueline.com), or Computerized Portfolio Management Services (www.cpms.com). Each of these programs offers a user-friendly method to scan for qualified stocks using either their predetermined screens or your own set of criteria. You can also test the effectiveness of a screen by using the software's built-in back tester. Once you create a list of screened stocks, you can do further diligence on them before committing to a software purchase.

A final thought about using automated stock screening software. As good as it is, it won't replace all of your hard work. You still need to do further research on the stocks that the software picks, for example, by reading news stories and independent research service reports. Through diligent effort, you can develop and follow an effective and profitable equity-management process.

In a Nutshell

Once you become comfortable with candlestick charting, you will never go back to standard bar charts. Candlesticks are useful both as a stand-alone short-term timing tool and (preferably) in conjunction with the analytical methods taught in this book. Use candlesticks to help you identify significant market movements.

The concept of candlestick charting is simple to understand. Black candles represent lower closes. White candles represent higher closes. Bigger real bodies mean larger swings on up or down days. In a single glance at a candlestick chart, you can recognize a series of large white candles vividly illustrating the prevailing bullish mood of the crowd. Conversely, a series of large black candles can instantly identify strongly bearish momentum. The significance of engulfing patterns, hammers, and stars are pretty straightforward. They are easily recognizable on your chart once you've committed the patterns to memory.

Make a point to learn these simple patterns. You'll not regret it. Remember, you are always looking for an edge to support your trading success. Candlestick pattern recognition may just provide it.

Most candlestick patterns help you identify reversal points. There are also continuation patterns within candlestick charts. I've focused in this chapter on the most common candlestick reversal patterns and omitted coverage of candlestick continuation patterns. In my opinion, the latter are less useful than the traditional pennant and flag continuation patterns described in chapter 3 of this book. There are many more candlestick patterns. If you're interested in using candlestick analysis to a greater degree in your own technical analysis, get and study Steve Nison's book, mentioned earlier.

In our next and final chapter, we'll pull everything that I've taught you together. We'll analyze the market from a macro-trend perspective and then work our way down to making a series of buy and sell decisions based on individual sectors and security selections.

8

PULLING IT ALL TOGETHER

IN this chapter I present the steps you should take to make profitable entry and exit decisions on the stock markets. In my capacity as Portfolio Manager for my firm, ValueTrend Wealth Management, I am responsible for providing my clients an acceptable rate of return with as little risk as possible. The process taught in this book comes to |you directly from the real world of trading. Every tool presented in the chapters of *Sideways* I have used successfully in real-time money management in my practice. This book offers a hard-nosed and practical guide in comparison with the conceptual approach taught by many financial advice books.

I hope to impart this pragmatic, step-by-step approach to you to increase your odds of a profitable, lower risk portfolio.

Let's begin by taking a brief look at three steps you can take when formulating your investment strategy. I'll expand on these steps as we progress through the chapter.

Step One: Broad Market Analysis

Step one is to take a top-down, or macro, view of the overall market environment. Phases and cycles, discussed previously, affect the broader markets as well as the individual securities that you're studying.

Identify these phases and cycles and reduce your exposure to equities when the broader picture is bearish (for example, if you identify a potential phase three topping pattern or the market has reached the seasonal selling period).

Increase your exposure to equities when your analysis points to a bullish market (for example, after identifying a phase one bottom pattern, or during an uptrend, or in the seasonal buying period).

After identifying the current phase and cycle of the market as a potential buying opportunity, examine the potential longevity and strength of the market. This is done by reviewing market breadth, market sentiment, and the current value of the markets as discussed in previous chapters.

Step Two: Confirmation

Let's assume you're convinced that the outlook for the market is bullish. The next step is to analyze the finer details of the patterns, trends, and cycles that you have identified in step one. Momentum indicators and candlestick analysis will help you confirm the legitimacy of your observations both for the broader markets and for the individual sectors and securities you plan to trade.

Step Three: Individual Securities

Finally, in a bull market, look for individual securities that appear to offer good risk versus reward within the broader market observations you make. Estimate the approximate upside target versus the estimated downside risk of individual securities to help confirm entry decisions.

Introducing Sammy Stockpicker

As I did in my first book, *SmartBounce*, I'm going to use a fictional character to illustrate a step-by step process to analyze the markets. Let's call our investor Sammy Stockpicker.

Sammy Stockpicker's investment history throughout the sideways market that began in 1999 can be described as "been there, done that."

In the late 1990s, Sammy dealt with stockbrokers who recommended portfolios of stocks from their firms' recommended lists. Sammy was distressed as he watched the broker make plenty of commissions while his portfolio floundered. He told his broker that he wanted better results from his portfolio. His stockbroker suggested that perhaps they should shy away from buying stocks and bonds directly. She recommended a few mutual funds plus an in-house managed wrap-account product.

After several years of watching his managed products portfolio rise and fall with the markets, Sammy decided he'd be no worse off if he managed his investments on his own.

Sammy moved his account away from the big brokerage firm to a discount brokerage. He heard about two investment newsletters and decided to subscribe. These supposedly respected publications were written by gurus and market pundits who bragged about their publications' great track record. For some reason, Sammy never achieved big returns by following their recommendations. Perhaps the publications were printed too late for Sammy to buy the recommended stocks at the prices they suggested.

In frustration, Sammy began following the financial media. He felt that by listening to a wide variety of opinions he might be able to choose from a number of investment ideas on a timely basis. Sammy figured that investment specialists smart enough to be featured in the national media surely must be good at what they do.

Acting on the "stock du jour" recommendations of a variety of investment managers and talking heads featured in the media didn't help Sammy's steadily dwindling portfolio. He began to wonder if these experts were just trying to pump up stocks they already owned.

Sammy participated in every investment bubble since he began investing in the late 1990s. He plunged head-first into the hype that surrounded the technology bubble of the late 1990s with the help of his stockbroker of the time. He overloaded his portfolio with technology stocks and info-tech mutual funds. He swore he would never again be caught in an investment bubble.

Sammy bought into apparently safe income trusts through the early to mid 2000s when he left his stockbroker and started investing on his own. Income trusts were paying high tax-advantaged distributions to unit holders. They were advancing in price aggressively at the time. As is always the case when something is too good to be true, in the fall of 2006 the Canadian Finance minister announced that, by 2011, income trusts would no longer be the easy ride that investors had been enjoying. The news caused this overhyped and little-understood trust sector to implode immediately after the announcement. Sammy's portfolio sank like a stone.

The commodity bubble of the late 2000s saw Sammy buying commodity stocks and ETFs while chanting the mantra "oil to $200 a barrel." Sammy, who should have known by then how to spot the makings of an investment bubble, watched his portfolio lose almost all of the progress he had made toward recovering from his previous investment mistakes.

All along the way, of course, Sammy owned plenty of stocks, like his buddies, looking to profit through compelling stories of "the next big thing."

Sammy hasn't had much luck in his investment career. Luckily, he happened on the manuscript of *Sideways* in early 2010 and decided to diligently apply its disciplined and analytical investment approach.

Following the rigorous approach outlined in *Sideways* has involved more time and effort than his past investment sorties. But the results have been worth it. Sammy feels comfortable with both the returns and the risk controls he's put into place since gaining a better understanding of the phases and trends of the markets.

Let's sit next to Sammy today as he analyzes the current state of the markets and decides his current investment moves.

Sammy Analyzes the Broad Markets for Trend and Confirmation

Back in April 2010, Sammy had sold a number of his equity positions to reduce his equity portfolio exposure by 40% from his previous fully-invested level. The decision to reduce his equity exposure was made in light of a few factors taken from lessons taught in *Sideways*.

After reading *Sideways*, Sammy was aware of the ultimate trading range top in the Dow 12000 area. Beyond its brief rise into the 14000 area in 2007, the market had been unable to break and remain much above the 12000 mark since 1999. Sammy was worried that the markets could face a potentially weaker period due to the overhead resistance at Dow 12000.

The Dow had broken through 11000 by mid-April. The crowd was bullish as corporate America delivered inspiring earnings reports. The Dow looked to be breaking a rising trendline, signifying a phase two bull market that had begun in March of 2009. Coincident to the Dow soaring through 11000 (before it penetrated its trendline) was the pending end of the Best Six Months seasonal strategy. Sammy had read that this strategy triggered investors to reduce equity by May of every year as the end of the strongest six months (November to April) approached.

Another factor that inspired Sammy to take a more cautious stance was a high reading on the Shiller PE ratio. By the third week of April, the Shiller PE ratio sat at almost 23. That was at the high end of its historic trading range. This indicated a potentially overvalued market. Interestingly, both the ISEE sentiment index, with readings of 160 or higher throughout April, and the RSI momentum oscillator, also with readings of over 70 for much of April, had reached overbought levels at that time. Putting all of these factors together, Sammy decided that a market correction was overdue.

Given that the market had been rising on strong breadth, as indicated by a confirming A/D line, Sammy didn't feel the market was due for a massive crash or bear market just yet. He felt it would more likely be a "go nowhere" market that wouldn't offer too many trading opportunities over the next six months.

This sideways pattern may eventually break out to the upside for a new leg of the bull market, but Sammy was also aware that a breakout to the downside would likely signal a new bear market.

Sammy sold his broad-market ETFs such as those representing the S&P 500 and TSX 60 indices. He also sold the energy-stocks that he had in the portfolio since buying them in February, the seasonally favorable time to buy the energy sector. He sold a couple of other stocks that he noticed had a high correlation to the stock market's movements. He held the proceeds of these sales in short-termed treasury bills. Sammy remembered reading about why correlation matters. Stocks that perform in sync with the broader market movements are vulnerable to market weakness.

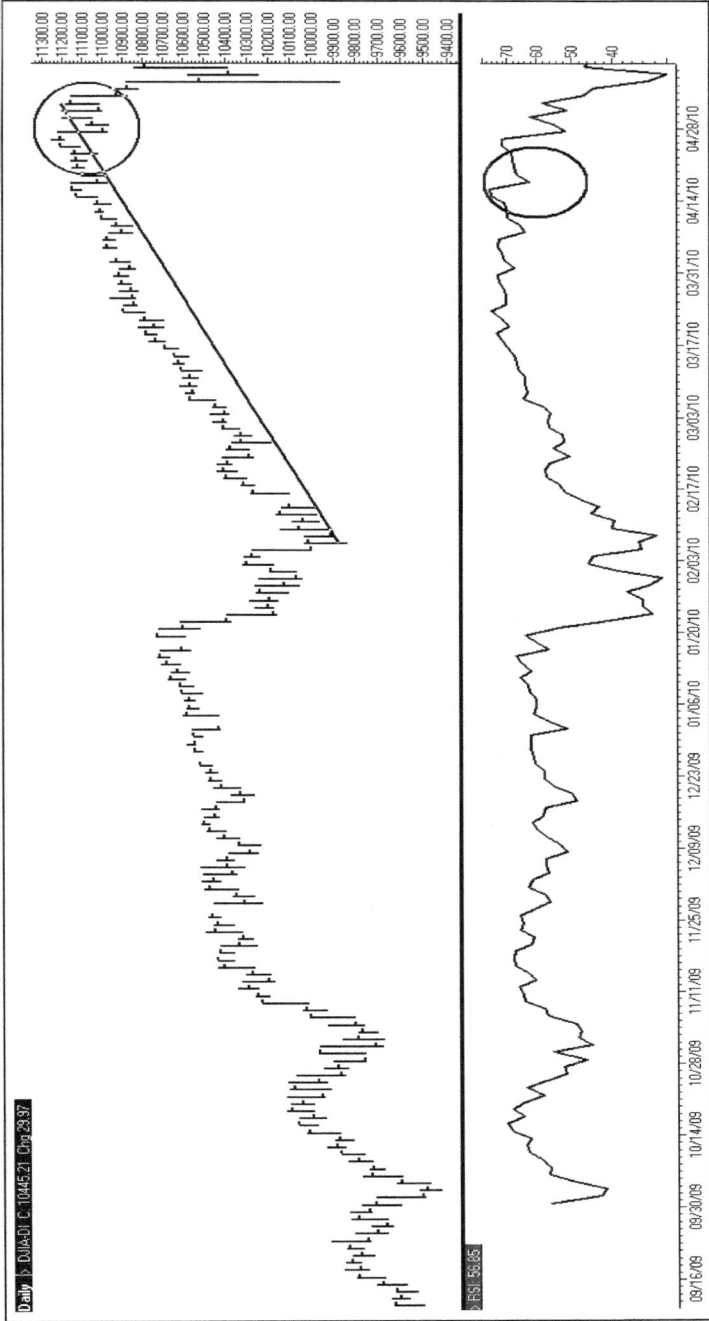

Figure 45. Chart of the Dow September 2009 to April 2010 with RSI. Overbought RSI readings above 70 (circled) coincided with the Dow approaching its 11500 technical resistance, a high Shiller PE ratio, and the breaking of a trendline that had been in place since February 2010. Note the market's retracement immediately after these factors were identified. (Copyright © 1988–2008 Thomson Financial)

PULLING IT ALL TOGETHER

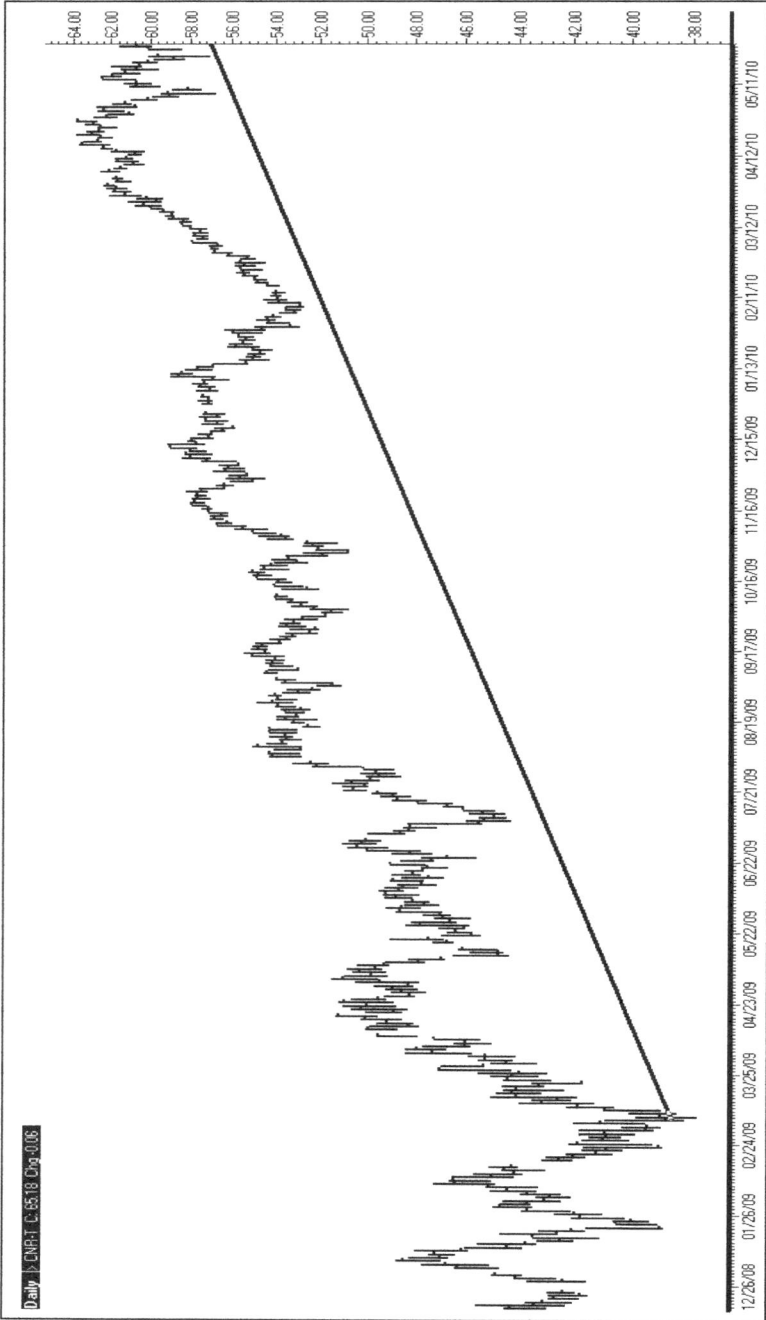

Figure 46. Chart of CN Railway December 2008 to May 2010 with trendline. (Copyright © 1988-2008, Thomson Financial)

Sammy Looks for Individual Securities

Sammy also rotated out of his consumer discretionary ETF and into a consumer staples ETF. He previously confirmed that the consumer staples ETF demonstrated a bullish-looking double-bottom pattern on a daily chart. He checked his remaining stocks to determine how they had held out during other market corrections. He wanted to hold only stocks that had fallen about half of what the market had fallen during past corrections. To do this, he simply measured peak to trough drawdowns on his existing stocks.

Then he noted how long it took for his positions to recover after a drawdown. Sammy also drew support lines where his stocks had dipped and bounced up in the past. This was to estimate the likely downside potential in the event of a market correction. Ideally, stocks with less than half of the downside volatility during the 2008-2009 correction were desirable.

CN Rail was one stock that met these criteria. It had a peak-to-trough drawdown of about 20% versus the TSX's 60% total drawdown during the same period. The stock price was also keeping well above a trendline that was established in March 2008. So Sammy felt comfortable holding CNR.

Back to the Broad Market Analysis

Sammy kept the cash from his April selloff through most of the summer. By late July, he noticed that gold was retreating enough to bring it close to its former support level. This coincided beautifully with the traditional seasonal buying window for gold and gold stocks. Sammy bought a gold stock ETF with a portion of the cash in his investment account. He still kept a large amount of cash on the sidelines.

Not surprisingly, the stock market gyrated up and down through the summer. Sammy noted that each time the markets rallied after a selloff, the volume declined as market prices went up. Sammy recalled from reading *Sideways* that one way to test the strength of conviction in a market movement is through confirmation of volume. If volume doesn't increase when the market is moving sharply in a given direction, it probably means the movement will not last.

The low trading volume on market rallies during the summer suggested conviction behind these movements was low. Sammy noticed, more often than not, a trend for the markets to give up some of the gains they made

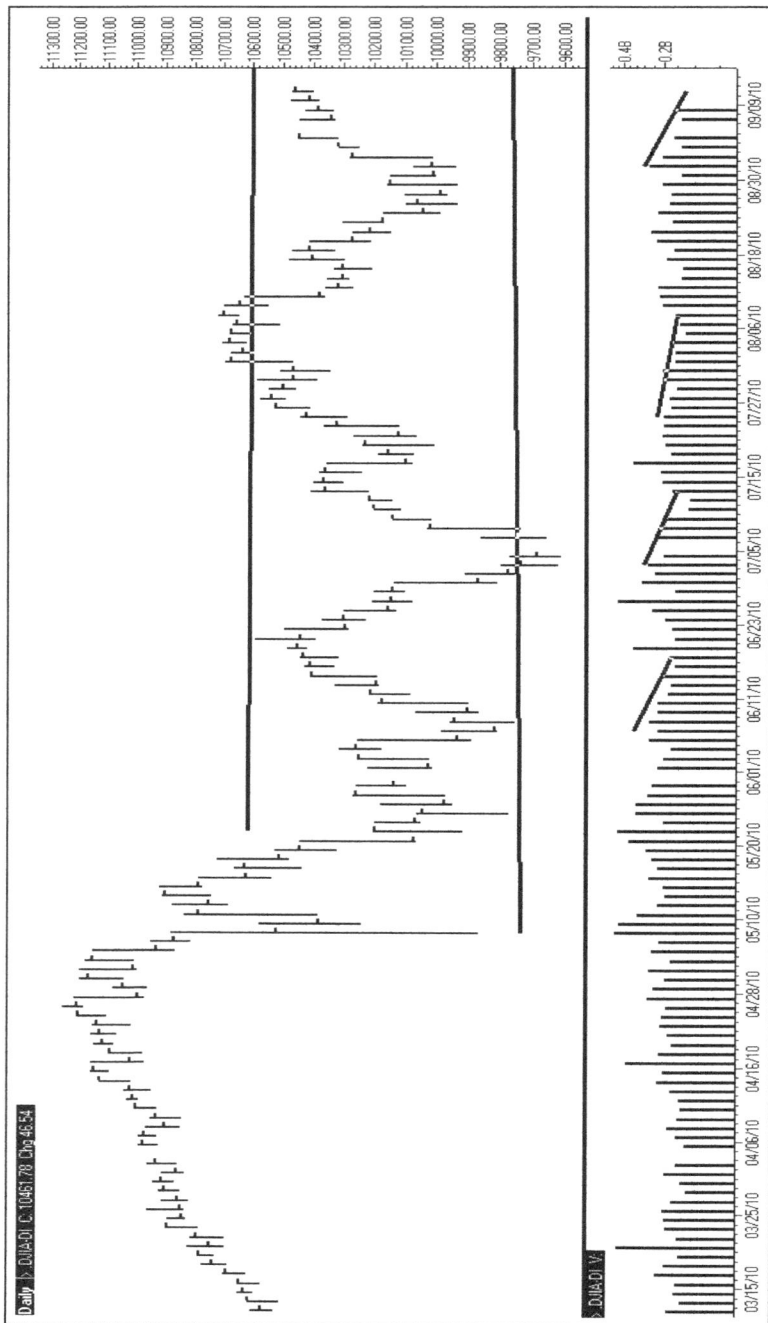

Figure 47. Dow, summer of 2010. Note the sideways trading range and low volume rallies. (Copyright © 1988-2008, Thomson Financial)

during the day in the last couple of hours of trading. The smart money was taking profit at the end of the day. The volume patterns suggested that many traders were sitting on the sidelines, not buying stocks.

Sammy felt comfortable staying in cash, gold, and low volatility equities until the start of the Best Six Months seasonal cycle in the late fall. He would watch for a strong market selloff around late October or so. That might present an opportunity to get back into the markets with his cash. Perhaps the Dow would approach the low end of its summer trading range, which was around 9700 (see figure 47, page 108).

Sammy watched the markets break out of the summer's sideways trading pattern in late September. Seasonal patterns can often be bearish for September and October, so he decided to wait until November before reinvesting the cash he had held over the summer. The market had been rising in September and October in anticipation of an important stimulation announcement by the U.S. Federal Reserve on November 3, 2010. Technical indicators such as RSI and the ISE put/call ratio were suggesting that excitement over the upcoming Fed meeting was overblown. Markets looked overbought. One week after the Fed announced an important stimulus package for the economy, the Dow finally pulled back several hundred points from its drastically overbought levels. Sammy felt this was the time to act.

Sammy sold half his gold holdings. He had watched gold realize a solid return from his mid-summer purchase price. Gold's seasonal period of strength usually ended in the fall. Despite the uptrend still being in place, he felt it was a smart move to take at least some of his profit and run.

He entered the stock market using the cash he had held over the summer by buying both U.S. and Canadian broad index ETFs. He also swapped his consumer staples ETF out of the portfolio by buying a consumer discretionary ETF with the proceeds. Sammy knew the information technology sector entered its strong seasonal period in October. He performed a computerized scan for individual technology stocks that fit his criteria for companies with strong balance sheets and a solid earnings growth history. From the list produced by his computer scan, Sammy purchased shares in a stock that looked to be entering into a phase two uptrend after breaking out of a phase one rectangular consolidation pattern.

Sammy looks back

Sammy continued to exercise the discipline instilled in him through reading *Sideways*. He reduced his portfolio risk in the spring by taking profits when markets appeared less attractive. He bought back into equities when markets appeared more attractive in the fall by following a disciplined seasonal approach.

Sammy is no longer a victim of the emotional swings of the markets. He now uses tools to prosper in today's volatile markets.

RESOURCES

RECOMMENDED READING

Appel, Gerald. *Beat the Market: Win with Proven Stock Selection and Market Timing Tools.*

Boeckh, Anthony. *The Great Reflation: How Investors Can Profit from the New World of Money.*

Bulkowski, Thomas N. *Encyclopedia of Chart Patterns.*

Edwards, Robert D., John Magee, and W.H. Charles Bassetti. *Technical Analysis of Stock Trends.*

Elder, Alexander. *Trading For a Living: Psychology, Trading Tactics, Money Management.*

Frost, A.J. and Robert Prechter. *Elliott Wave Principle: Key to Market Behavior.*

Hirsch, Jeffrey. *Stock Trader's Almanac 2011* (Almanac Investor Series).

Hurst, J.M. *The Profit Magic of Stock Transaction Timing.*

Murphy, John J. *Technical Analysis of the Futures Markets: A Comprehensive Guide to Trading Methods and Applications.*

Neill, Humphrey Bancroft. *The Art of Contrary Thinking.*

Prechter, Robert R. Jr. *The Wave Principle of Human Social Behavior and the New Science of Socioeconomics.*

Pring, Martin. *Martin Pring on Market Momentum.*

Pring, Martin. *Technical Analysis Explained: The Successful Investor's Guide to Spotting Investment Trends and Turning Points.*

Richards, Keith G. *SmartBounce: 3 Action Steps to Portfolio Recovery.*

Thackray, Brooke. *Thackray's 2011 Investor's Guide: How to Profit from Seasonal Market Trends.*

Weinstein, Stan. *Stan Weinstein's Secrets of Profiting in Bull and Bear Markets.*

Williams, Larry. *The Right Stock at the Right Time: Prospering in the Coming Good Years.*

RECOMMENDED WEBSITES

dvtechtalk.com
Don Vialoux's free technical analysis website, featuring seasonal, fundamental, and technical analysis of the stock market from a respected Technical Analyst.

Sentimentrader.com
Offers a huge variety of sentiment indicators to subscribers including excellent daily market commentary.

Vectorvest.com
Quantitative fundamental analysis tool for screening stocks.

Ise.com
Free call/put sentiment indicator

Strategicanalysis.ca
Unique analysis of corporate balance sheets.

Freestockcharts.com
Great free charting software that does almost everything the costly charting software does.

Stockcharts.com
John Murphy's charting site offers quick and easy free charting, or advanced charting for subscribers.

SmartBounce.ca
Keith G. Richards' technical analysis blog.

Multpl.com
Free charts of various long-term fundamental ratios.

Thechartstore.com
Low-cost subscription gives you a huge number of unique and valuable charts.

Bnn.ca
Business News Network Television website features clips of BNN shows throughout the day.

CPSIA information can be obtained at www.ICGtesting.com
Printed in the USA
LVOW010341200912

299505LV00009B/14/P